COMPUTERS AND DATA PROCESSING MADE SIMPLE

CALVIN A. HOFEDITZ

MADE SIMPLE BOOKS
DOUBLEDAY & COMPANY, INC.
GARDEN CITY, NEW YORK

Library of Congress Cataloging in Publication Data

Hofeditz, Calvin A
Computers and data processing made simple.

(Made simple books)
1. Electronic digital computers. 2. Electronic
data processing. I. Title.
QA76.5.H598   001.6′4
ISBN: 0-385-14945-X
Library of Congress Catalog Card Number 78–22635

CONTENTS

INTRODUCTION /7

UNIT 1 THE FUNDAMENTALS /15

UNIT 2   THE COMPUTER /54

UNIT 3   THE INSTRUCTIONS /70

UNIT 4   THE PROGRAMS /88

UNIT 5   THE SYSTEMS /107

ANSWERS TO UNIT QUIZZES /125

GLOSSARY OF TERMS /133

FIGURES

TABLES

INTRODUCTION

If you are a typical American, you've probably blamed computers for making mistakes in your utility bills, producing the wrong address in address labels on mail you receive, and failing to keep charge or checking accounts accurate. These are all minor irritations we've lived with for years. Most of these mistakes are caused by human error, however, and are not the result of a computer failure. After you've read this book you'll understand that computer failures are easily detected, but the human errors made in supplying data to the machines and in using them are not.

In the 1950s, when electronic computers of the nature we are using today were being developed, the cost of a machine was very high, running into hundreds of thousands of dollars for the large machines. In addition, their size and reliability were such that large staffs of supporting personnel were required to keep the equipment operating. That has all changed. Computing power is now portable and cheap, and it is rapidly becoming more compact and cheaper.

As of this writing, in the fall of 1978, the major retailers are beginning to offer small computers for home use, along with the instructions for programming and using them. We can expect to see this product grow like many others, developing the need for new services. The sales of electronic games designed to be attached to the TV receiver are measures of both the acceptance and the versatility of a computer. These games are controlled by microcomputers within their control units.

Knowledge of what computers do and how they do it is important to us all. The operator of a small business, for example, may find the cost of his record-keeping going up rapidly and consider using a computer to do the job. Large companies can employ specialists to select computers and services, while the small-businessman must make the choices himself. When computer sales representatives call, this man may be confronted with a bewildering array of machines and computer-industry jargon used by the salesmen. Unless he has some knowledge of what computers do and their capabilities and limitations, he runs the risk of buying or leasing equipment ill suited to his job and possibly making his record-keeping system even more expensive.

For those considering careers in the computer and data-processing industry, it is important to know what they are getting into. In general, a good deal of training is required for the jobs available, and at least some of it is "dry" and mathematical in nature. Many of the jobs involve long hours at a desk in an office. After a reader has completed this book, he should know whether a job in the computer industry is likely to please him.

Many people now working at jobs in which computers are used know only a little about what the machines do for them. Data-processing orders come from the supervisor, the machines are reprogrammed, new equipment is installed, and technicians make repairs. All these activities would have more meaning to these computer users if they knew more about the internal workings of the machines. This could make their jobs more interesting as well as lead to advancement.

Last, why should the layman who has no direct contact with computers need to know how they work? Nearly everyone's life is affected to some extent by today's use of computers, and this will increase in the future. Nearly all people are also potential customers for a computer or a computer service, as they were for radios, television receivers, and small calculators. Most people feel familiar with the terms used to describe what these units do and would not hesitate to discuss the replacement of a tube in their TV set with a TV repairman. A similar familiarity with the use of computers will be necessary soon, if it is not now, and this book will provide a base on which to build.

WHERE COMPUTERS ARE USED

Most of us associate computers with numbers and immediately relate computers and businesses dealing with numbers, such as accounting departments and banks. Repetitive numerical tasks are natural applications of computers, but most accounting departments and banks were already "computerized" before electronic computers arrived. They used mechanical adding machines and electromechanical equipment such as card sorters for many years.

Management of telephone switching systems is an application of computers that most of us don't think of much. But it too is a "natural." Two telephone numbers must be connected quickly. With its ability to manipulate numbers, make decisions, and turn connections on and off with great speed, the electronic computer is easily adapted to control telephone switching systems.

Process control is a task ranging from the management of fluid flow in oil refineries to operation of machine tools. It too is a major application of electronic computers. The problem here is that the computer must be fitted with "senses" to "see and feel" the processes taking place. Its "senses" must provide it with numbers. Then the computer must have a way in which it can "touch" the process in order to convert its numbers into action.

These "senses" and "hands" are electromechanical units. Consider the operation of a machine tool whose function is cutting, as an example. First, the computer is provided with an indication that the stock to be cut is in place, and the cutting blade is fully retracted. The computer then supplies numbers to the blade controller, causing it to move the blade forward in small increments and, in return, the computer is provided with numbers indicating the blade's position. Stored in its memory, the computer holds a number that represents the limit to which the blade is to travel. Continually comparing the current blade position with the travel limit, the computer moves the blade until that limit is reached. The computer then considers that process complete and moves on to the next cut to be made. There is virtually no limit to the accuracy that the computer can provide; the limitation lies in the accuracy of the electromechanical units at the point at which the process takes place.

An example of such process control could be computer-controlled lathes in a furniture factory. Assume that there were five such machines making chair legs. Only one operator would be required to turn on the machines, to put the stock in place, and to remove the finished legs. Every leg would be identical, regardless of the operator's skill, and the cost should be considerably lower than if five skilled machinists were required to operate the same lathes.

As computers become ever smaller and cheaper they find more applications. Most readers have seen the electronic cash registers used in retail stores but do not fully appreciate what these machines do. Adding of merchandise sales and calculating change were easily done by the old mechanical cash registers. Of course, the electronic machines do that, but they also do much more. Located deep within these machines is a small computer, and it is usually linked to a larger computer located elsewhere in the store. When a merchandise code and the number of these items sold is entered by the clerk, the cash register's computer forwards this information to the large machine. In turn, the larger computer looks up the merchandise code and deducts the number of items sold from the total in stock. So the store knows at all times the number of these items it has left for sale.

To carry this one step farther, the larger computer can be set so as to automatically place a purchase order to replenish the stock when the inventory is reduced to a certain level. If this computer is linked to a supplier's computer, the order can be sent and acknowledged electronically. In turn, the supplier's computer knows what his inventory level is, and whether or not the order can be filled immediately. It informs the retail store of the delivery date and prepares production and shipping orders at the supplier's plant.

These are only a few representative applications of general-purpose computers. They were chosen because they deal with processes that a reader can easily visualize. Computers guide and control spacecraft and missiles, control bill-paying by telephone, prepare your paycheck, and play electronic games with you on the television screen. (Some readers may have had the computer also play electronic games with their paycheck.)

USES IN THE FUTURE

Reduction in size and cost of supporting units are the key factors in the spread of computers. The computer itself can already be made very small, but such things as a display screen, keyboard, tape drives, and printers necessary to provide the inputs and display the outputs are still fairly large and costly.

Construction of the computer's "senses" required for process control mentioned above is also complex and costly. When microcomputers appear in automobiles to control some engine functions, the most costly portion of the system will be the equipment necessary to adapt the computer to its task, not the computer itself.

Another important factor that can hold back computer use is the availability of computer programs that meet the require-

ments of each application. The electronic games serve to illustrate this. One can buy cheaply a set of certain game programs. Others could be prepared by the manufacturer, but each is costly to prepare and thus only those that can be sold in large numbers are written. The same is true of programs prepared for general-purpose computers applied to business problems. Differences in methods of inventory control may make a program prepared for one business nearly useless for another. This requires that each business buy a "tailored suit" rather than an "off the rack" version. Needless to say, this runs up the cost of applying the computer and makes it less attractive. The high-level programming languages discussed in Unit 4 help some in keeping down programming costs. All, however, still require considerable training in their use and must be advanced before being offered for sale to the public.

One computer application that the reader can expect to see in the near future is an electronic funds transfer system, which is already beginning to take shape in some areas. Since the banking system is now well equipped with computers and the post office is burdened with high costs and a very large volume of mail, a logical conclusion is to eliminate checks and bills and to transfer funds between accounts electronically, providing only a monthly record of the transfers. The electronic deposit of regularly issued government payments (such as Social Security payments) into the payee's account is where this system will probably be seen first.

Computer-aided medical diagnosis is another area in which computer use will spread and be immediately visible to the layman. One can expect to find a small computer terminal in a doctor's office, which is linked to a large computer in a nearby hospital. When the results of tests made by the medical staff, the patient's history, and answers provided to computer questions are analyzed by the machine, further tests and probable causes can quickly be suggested by the computer. This can be done much faster by the computer than it can be by the medical staff.

COMPUTER INDUSTRY CAREERS

All the jobs in the computer industry can be grouped into the following five categories:

a. Designing and building the machines
b. Preparing the computer programs
c. Applying the machines and programs to specific jobs
d. Operating and using the computer systems
e. Maintaining and repairing the systems

The degree of training required ranges from operator training, which is a maximum of a few weeks, to that needed by programmers and designers. A four-year college degree is usually required for the most difficult design and programming jobs.

One has only to look in employment sections of the newspapers in major cities to evaluate the demand for data processing and computer specialists and the salaries available. The demand obviously exceeds the supply now, and many companies provide lengthy training courses to promising candidates. Most two-year colleges also offer a broad range of computer-related courses that lead directly to jobs.

Don't get the idea that all jobs in this industry are interesting, fascinating, and glamorous; many are not. But they do usually offer pleasant working conditions and pay well. Most require that you work in an office environment and deal with a lot of paperwork, although the operation and maintenance jobs are less likely to.

CONTENTS OF THIS BOOK

This book is written for those who have had little or no experience with computers. It describes what computers do, generally how they do it, and how they are programmed and used. In order to present the material in the order that the reader would normally use it, five units of information have been organized. Each is accompanied by a quiz to aid in studying the material. Answers are given at the back of the book.

Unit 1, "The Fundamentals," is by far the largest unit. It deals with the basic processes that computers must perform and identifies the elements of computers and computer systems.

Unit 2 is entitled "The Computer." It shows how the elements of a computer are constructed and how they operate both internally and with one another.

Unit 3, "The Instructions," is next. All computers perform instructions one after another in a logical order. Unit 3 describes all the instructions that a typical computer can perform.

Unit 4 is called "The Programs." A group of instructions arranged so as to make the computer do a specific job is called a program. What programs are like and how they are prepared are covered in this unit.

Unit 5, "The Systems," shows how a computer and its programs operate together. A typical installation is shown and a payroll-preparation operation is described to illustrate computer applications.

At the end of the book, you'll find a Glossary of Terms. It gives a description not only of terms used in Units 1 through 5 but also many of the other terms used throughout the computer industry.

COMPUTERS AND
DATA PROCESSING
MADE SIMPLE

UNIT 1

THE FUNDAMENTALS

"OPEN THIS END" is a notice that most of us have seen on cartons when it is important that the contents be removed carefully and in a certain order. A similar notice could be applied to this book. The reader must have a clear understanding of the material given in Unit 1, "The Fundamentals," before moving on to Units 2 through 5, and the following is a brief description of what the reader will find in this unit.

Unit 1 opens with a description of numbering systems used by computers. Introduced here are three numbering systems (binary, octal, and hexadecimal) that many readers may be encountering for the first time, yet they must be used often by all who work closely with computers.

Nearly all computer operations, no matter how complex, are performed by six very simple elements: ANDs, ORs, NANDs, NORs, inverters, and bi-stables. These elements are used in very large numbers even in small computers, so a brief description of each element and its function appears early in Unit 1.

Next, a section entitled "Binary Arithmetic" shows the reader how to combine what he has learned about the binary numbering

system and the basic elements to perform the addition and subtraction of numbers just as it is done within a computer. While most will never find it necessary to do binary arithmetic with pencil and paper, this section adds to their knowledge of what is happening inside a computer.

How data is organized for and by the computer is discussed next in Unit 1. Bytes, records, files, and volumes are introduced and described.

Unit 1 then shifts to a discussion of components that make up a computer. The reader will find that the expression "If you've seen one, you've seen 'em all" does apply to the organization of general-purpose computers. Big or small, they all have the same five basic units in their architecture.

"Peripherals" is a term used widely in the computer industry. It means the units that are used with the computer but that are not part of the basic machine. The purpose and characteristics of each peripheral unit (which includes magnetic tapes, disk units, and printers) are discussed in the conclusion of Unit 1.

A DESCRIPTION OF NUMBERING SYSTEMS

Most readers have given very little thought to any numbering system other than the decimal system they use daily. Computers use only the binary numbering system, how-

ever, and it is necessary to understand this system before becoming familiar with the internal operations of data-processing equipment.

The Binary System

There are only two characters in the binary system: 0 and 1. For this reason, binary is well suited to digital computers. Most electronic components used in computers have only two stable states, on and off. By associating 0 with off and 1 with on, this bistable nature of electrical devices can easily represent the two characters of the binary system.

Decimal Notation	Binary Notation
	4 2
	8 ↓↓↓↓ 1
0	0000
1	0001
2	0010
3	0011
4	0100
5	0101
6	0110
7	0111
8	1000
9	1001
10	1010
11	1011
12	1100
13	1101
14	1110
15	1111

In order to explain how counting takes place in the binary system, it is necessary to briefly review the concept of "positional notation." Familiar to all are the "units," "tens," "hundreds," "thousands," etc., positions in the decimal numbering system. When one of the ten possible decimal characters (0 through 9) is placed in the rightmost place of a whole number, it represents "units," in the next position "tens," and so forth. The same positional notation scheme is used in the binary system except that the positions are "units," "twos," "fours," etc.,

with each position doubling the value of the position to its right instead of increasing by ten times, as in the decimal system. This is because the binary system has a base of two characters rather than ten. Assume that a four-place binary number is to be converted to decimal form for easy reading. The table to the left illustrates how that is done. A numerical value in decimal is assigned to each position in the binary number, ranging from "1" in the least significant position to "8" in the most significant position. If a binary 1 occupies that position, it represents the decimal value assigned to that position.

Converting Binary Numbers to Other Systems

Methods used to convert from binary to decimal and decimal back to binary are covered in many publications, and it is beyond the scope of this discussion to cover them in detail here. Conversion is rather time-consuming for large numbers and, for that reason, it is generally not done manually. Computer programs accept the decimal input and provide the decimal output, relieving the user of that task.

For small numbers, the conversion is rather simple. The decimal value is assigned to each binary position, doubling with each position as shown in the example above. In converting from binary to decimal, the user simply reads each "1" in the binary number as the decimal value of that position and adds up the decimal numbers to acquire the value of the binary number.

To convert from decimal to binary, the user writes out the decimal values of each binary position and places 1s in the appropriate positions. For example, assume that the decimal number 125 is to be converted to binary. This requires the following steps:

a. Write out the binary positions 1, 2, 4, 8, 16, 32, 64, and 128 until the binary position whose value is larger than that of the decimal number to be converted is reached.

b. Then start placing "1s" in the binary positions. Obviously a "0" must be placed in the "128" position.

c. Next, place a "1" in the "64" position and subtract 64 from 125, which leaves 61.

d. Place a "1" in the "32" position and subtract 32 from 61, leaving 29.

e. Place a "1" in the "16" position and subtract 16 from 29, leaving 13.

f. Place a "1" in the "8" position and subtract 8 from 13, leaving 5.

g. Place a "1" in the "4" position and subtract 4 from 5, leaving 1.

h. Place a "0" in the "2" position; then place a "1" in the "1" position to complete the conversion.

As illustrated in the preceding example, conversion between decimal and binary is slow and clumsy to do. Therefore, two other numbering systems, octal and hexadecimal, are commonly used in the data-processing industry.

Table 1. Relationship of Octal, Decimal, and Binary Systems

Decimal Notation	Octal Notation	Binary Notation
0	0	000
1	1	001
2	2	010
3	3	011
4	4	100
5	5	101
6	6	110
7	7	111
8	10	001 000
9	11	001 001
10	12	001 010
11	13	001 011
12	14	001 100
13	15	001 101
14	16	001 110
15	17	001 111
16	20	010 000

The Octal System

The octal system is essentially a shorthand method for replacing groups of three binary digits with a single octal digit. It uses eight characters, 0 through 7. Hence, each octal digit has eight times the weight of the next less significant digit to the right (octal digits increase by powers of eight). Table 1 below shows the manner in which octal numbers are formed.

Each binary position is assigned a value, just as in the binary to decimal system. Since this is still the binary system, the values double, 1 to 2 to 4. The difference is that each group of three binary positions repeats the 1-2-4 scheme rather than progressing to 8-16-32, etc. This makes it very easy to convert between octal and binary.

The Hexadecimal System

The hexadecimal system is a way of reading four binary positions as a single hexadecimal number. However, four binary digits can be arranged into 16 different combinations. Hence, the use of a four-bit code to represent decimals from 0 to 9 wastes six out of these possible sixteen combinations. In order not to waste the six unused combinations, notation in the scale of 16, or hexadecimal notation, is used in some computers. The hexadecimal system is a combination of the ten digits 0 to 9 and a choice of six letters of the alphabet, which are also treated as numbers. Table 2 shows the relationship between binary combinations and the hexadecimal system. The letters representing digits 10 to 15 are in alphabetical sequence A through F, or more descriptively, A for 10, B for 11, C for 12, D for 13, E for 14, and F for 15. Thus each of the symbols in the hexadecimal system exactly replaces one four-digit binary combination, permitting direct conversion.

Table 2. Relationship of Hexadecimal and Binary Systems

Binary Notation	Hexadecimal Notation
0000	0
0001	1
0010	2
0011	3
0100	4
0101	5
0110	6
0111	7
1000	8
1001	9
1010	A
1011	B
1100	C
1101	D
1110	E
1111	F

BASIC COMPUTER ELEMENTS

Since computers handle information in binary form, requiring only "on" and "off" conditions to represent a "1" and a "0," respectively, the basic circuits used are also simple. When combined in complex patterns, as they are in modern computers, these simple circuits are capable of performing highly sophisticated tasks, however.

Let's begin with the basic elements on which all computer operations are based. Their purpose is to manipulate and store binary numbers, and they include the following:

a. An OR gate, also called an OR circuit.
b. An AND gate, or AND circuit.
c. An inverter.
d. A bi-stable, most frequently called a flip-flop, but which is any device capable of assuming two distinct states.

Figure 1 shows the symbols used for each of these basic circuits. Inputs referred to in the following explanations are the lines on the left side of the symbol, and outputs are the lines on the right.

An OR gate may have two or more inputs. They are nearly unlimited in number, but four is a typical number. The rule for operation is: *If any one of the inputs is active, the output is active* regardless of the state of the other inputs.

It should be noted here that the values designated "active" or "inactive" vary from one manufacturer to another. With most circuits now widely used, however, "active" is the "1" and "high," while "inactive" is "0" and "low." In all the symbols shown in Figure 1, "L" is used to indicate a "low" (the inactive state), and "H" indicates a "high" (the active state).

An AND gate may have two or more inputs. Again, there is no limit on the number, but four inputs are typical. Its rule for operation is: *All inputs must be active for the output to be active.*

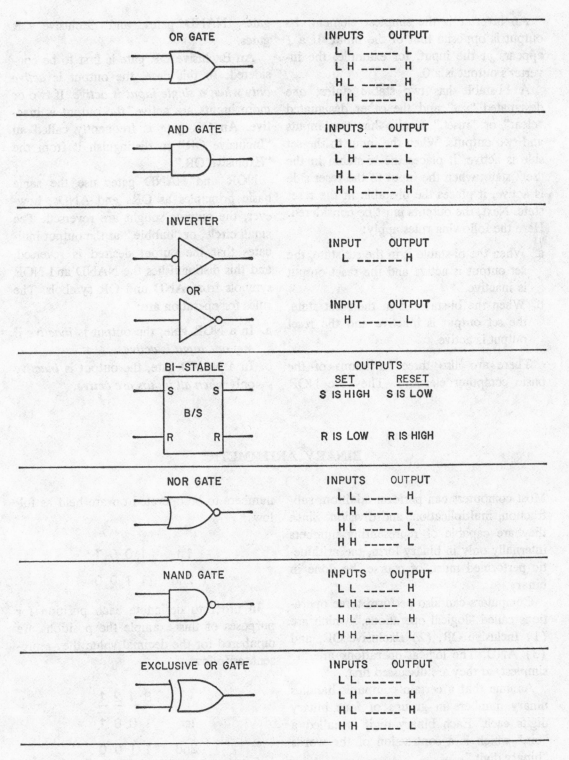

OR GATE	INPUTS	OUTPUT
	L L	L
	L H	H
	H L	H
	H H	H

AND GATE	INPUTS	OUTPUT
	L L	L
	L H	L
	H L	L
	H H	H

INVERTER	INPUT	OUTPUT
	L	H
OR	INPUT	OUTPUT
	H	L

BI-STABLE	OUTPUTS	
	SET	RESET
	S IS HIGH	S IS LOW
	R IS LOW	R IS HIGH

NOR GATE	INPUTS	OUTPUT
	L L	H
	L H	L
	H L	L
	H H	L

NAND GATE	INPUTS	OUTPUT
	L L	H
	L H	H
	H L	H
	H H	L

EXCLUSIVE OR GATE	INPUTS	OUTPUT
	L L	L
	L H	H
	H L	H
	H H	L

Figure 1. Symbols Used to Represent the Basic Computer Elements

An inverter is the simplest element. Its output is opposite that of the input. If a 1 appears at the input, for example, the inverter's output is a 0.

A bi-stable has two stable states, one designated "set" and the other designated "clear" or "reset." It also has two inputs and two outputs. When the input to the set side is active, it places the bi-stable in the "set" state; when the input to the reset side is active, it places the bi-stable in the reset state. Next, the outputs must be considered. Here the following rules apply:

a. When the bi-stable is in the set state, the set output is active and the reset output is inactive.

b. When the bi-stable is in the reset state, the set output is inactive and the reset output is active.

There are also three variations of the basic computer elements. They are NOR gates, NAND gates, and Exclusive OR gates.

An Exclusive OR gate is first to be considered. In this case, the output is *active only when a single input is active*. If two or more inputs are active, the output is inactive. An OR gate is frequently called an "Inclusive OR" to distinguish it from the "Exclusive OR."

NOR and NAND gates use the same basic principles as ORs and ANDs; however, the outputs sought are reversed. The small circle, or "bubble," at the output indicates that the output desired is reversed, and this distinguishes the NAND and NOR symbols from AND and OR symbols. The rules for operation are:

a. In a NOR gate, the output is *inactive* if any *one input is active*.

b. In a NAND gate, the output is *inactive* only *when all inputs are active*.

BINARY ARITHMETIC

Most computers can perform addition, subtraction, multiplication, and division. Since they are capable of representing numbers internally only in binary form, the arithmetic performed must, of course, be done in binary.

Computers can also perform three operations called "logical operations," which are (1) Inclusive OR, (2) Exclusive OR, and (3) AND. The logical operations are the simplest, so they are discussed first.

Assume that a certain computer handles binary numbers in groups of four binary digits each. Each binary digit is called a "bit," which is a contraction of the words "binary digit."

The first group of bits is 1001, and the second group, for purposes of this example, is 1100. Each group is held by a set of bi-stable elements discussed earlier. So the numbers to be operated on are held as follows:

1st	1 0 0 1
2nd	1 1 0 0

In order to designate each position for purposes of this example the positions are numbered for the decimal value they represent, as follows.

	8 4 2 1
1st	1 0 0 1
2nd	1 1 0 0

An Inclusive OR Operation

In this operation, each digit of the first group is matched with the corresponding digit of the second group. Where at least one of the digits is a "1," a "1" is placed in the result, as follows:

	8	4	2	1
1st	1	0	0	1
2nd	1	1	0	0
Result	1	1	0	1

An Exclusive OR Operation

In this operation, each digit of the first group is again matched with the corresponding digit of the second group. The result holds a "1" only when one of the digits is a "1" and the second is a "0," as follows:

	8	4	2	1
1st	1	0	0	1
2nd	1	1	0	0
Result	0	1	0	1

An AND Operation

When an AND operation is performed, each digit of the first group is matched with the corresponding digit of the second group. Both must be 1s in order for the result to be a 1, as follows:

	8	4	2	1
1st	1	0	0	1
2nd	1	1	0	0
Result	1	0	0	0

These logical operations are most commonly used to test or mask out portions of numbers. Their use will be illustrated in the discussion of typical instructions.

Addition

You'll notice that the logical operations shown above do not have carries from one bit position to another and, of course, addition requires carries in binary arithmetic just as it does in decimal arithmetic. The first point to be discussed, however, is the four possible combinations that can exist when two binary digits are added. These are shown below.

	A	B	C	D
	0	0	1	1
	+0	+1	+0	+1
Sum	0	1	1	0
Carry	0	0	0	1

Just as in the case of the decimal system, a carry to the next higher position must be produced when the capacity of a position to represent the result is exceeded. In the decimal system, each position can hold a number as high as 9, while in the binary system a 1 is the largest number a position can hold. So when the sum exceeds "1," a carry to the next position must be produced. This brings us to the combinations that can result when a given position has a carry in from the next lower position. These are shown below.

	A	B	C	D
	0	0	0	0
	+0	+0	+1	+1
Carry In	0	1	0	1
Sum	0	1	1	0
Carry Out	0	0	0	1

	E	F	G	H
	1	1	1	1
	+0	+0	+1	+1
Carry In	0	1	0	1
Sum	1	0	0	1
Carry Out	0	1	1	1

Next, apply the preceding principles to the addition of two four-place binary numbers:

16	8	4	2	1
1st		1	0	0	1
2nd +		1	1	0	0
Result (Sum)	1	0	1	0	1

Decimal Value

9

+12

21

The result has exceeded the capacity of four places, so the carry from the "8" position must go into the "16" position or be lost. In a computer dealing in only four-place binary numbers, this would be called an "overflow" condition. So the two four-place binary numbers to be added could not exceed a decimal total of 15. Normally the smallest number of positions in a computer would be 8, and there is no upper limit, although 64 positions is the maximum that would normally be used in a general-purpose computer.

Subtraction

Although it seems a contradiction in terms, subtraction is also done by addition. The difference is that one of the numbers, either the minuend or the subtrahend, is "complemented" first.

To "complement" in this case means to invert—that is, a "1" is changed to a "0" and a "0" to a "1" before the addition is performed, and the result is a subtraction. This is illustrated below.

	8	4	2	1
1st	1	1	0	0
2nd	+0	1	1	0
Result (Difference)	0	0	1	0

Decimal Value

12

−9 (a negative 9)

+ 2

A carry resulted from the "8" position. In subtraction, this is called an *end carry*, and it is brought back to the "1" position and added in, as follows:

	8	4	2	1
1st	1	1	0	0
2nd	+0	1	1	0
Difference	0	0	1	0
End Carry +				1
Final Difference	0	0	1	1

Decimal Value

12

−9 (a negative 9)

+3 (Final Difference)

The major disadvantage of subtraction carried out by this method is that two complete additions are required, the second being used to add the end carry, slowing the machine. Therefore, it is fairly common to represent negative numbers in what is called 2's complement form and to maintain a sign position that indicates whether the number is positive or negative. A 0 is most often used as the sign (+) for positive numbers and a 1 as the sign (−) for negative numbers.

Two's complement is a form in which a number is first complemented, as explained above, and then has a 1 added to it. For example:

	8	4	2	1
True form	1	0	0	1
Complemented	0	1	1	0
Two's complement	0	1	1	1

Decimal Value

9

−9 in 1's complement

−9 in 2's complement

Now return to the example in which 9 is to be subtracted from 12 and add as shown below:

	8	4	2	1
1st	1	1	0	0
2nd	+0	1	1	1
Result	0	0	1	1

Decimal Value

12

−9 in 2's complement

+ 3

An end carry from the position "8" stage is also produced under these circumstances, but it is discarded. Therefore, the second addition cycle is eliminated.

How a Computer Adds

The next step is to combine the principles of binary arithmetic given in the preceding paragraphs with the basic computer elements to show how a computer adder operates. Figure 2 illustrates the adder components necessary for each bit position. So far we have been dealing with only four-place numbers; there would be four complete sets of the components shown in Figure 2 in a computer handling four-place numbers. There would, of course, be thirty-two sets of these components if thirty-two-place numbers were handled by the machine. This serves to illustrate that the function performed by each of the basic computer elements is very simple and that a great many of these elements must be combined in order to perform useful work.

First to be discussed are the circuits that hold the numbers to be added. These are the two bi-stables in the upper left portion of the figure. When the bi-stables are combined into groups, they are called registers. In our case, we have one position of a register holding bit 1 of the first number and one position of another register holding bit 1 of the second number.

Bit 1 of the first number to be added is a "1"; therefore, its bi-stable is set. In turn, the "set" side output is active (high) and the "reset" side output is inactive (low).

Bit 1 of the second number to be added is a "0." Its bi-stable is thus in the reset condition, with its outputs opposite those of the first bi-stable.

In the next step, four AND gates combine the outputs of the bi-stables so as to determine which of four possible conditions exist for this bit position. We can see that we have two active (high) inputs to only AND gate B, so only AND gate B has an active output. It says "the sum of bit position 1 is a 1, and there is no carry from this position." Since the outputs of AND gates A, C, and D are all inactive, the conditions they represent do not exist.

The components shown in the upper portion of Figure 2 are often called a "half adder." They have not yet considered the possibility of a carry into bit position 1, so the final sum and carry have not yet been determined.

Across the lower section of the figure we have the rest of the adder. Two lines (carry in = 0, carry in = 1) represent the carry

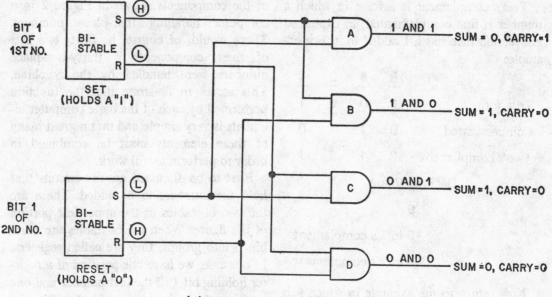

(a) FIRST HALF OF PROCESS

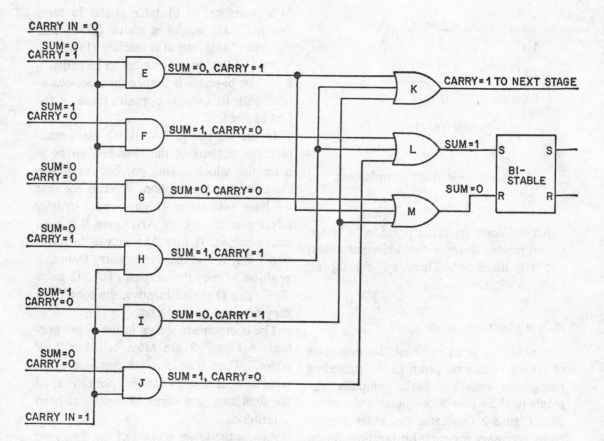

(b) SECOND HALF OF PROCESS

Figure 2. How a Computer Adds

from the previous stage. When a line is active, the condition it represents exists; when it is inactive, the condition does not exist.

Assume for the purpose of this explanation that the carry in = 0 line is active. Since we know that only the line from AND gate B (sum = 1, carry = 0) is active, this leaves us with active inputs to only AND gate F in the second portion of the adder. Its output thus becomes active to signify the final results for this position of the adder, which are: "Sum is a 1, and there is no carry out from this position."

OR gate K thus has no active inputs and does not produce the "carry = 1" signal to the next position. OR gate L has one active input, that being from AND gate F, signifying "sum = 1." This sets the bi-stable, recording the results for this bit position: a "sum = 1."

The operation just described has accomplished the following addition:

1st no.	1
2nd no.	0
Carry In	0
Sum	$\overline{1}$
Carry Out	0

A first impression the reader may gather is that a great many components are required to accomplish a very simple task. That is true, but the components are extremely small and fast. An 8-place adder, for example, occupies a space less than half that of a postage stamp, and performs the addition of two eight-bit numbers in only millionths of a second.

Multiplication

Multiplication is also performed by addition. For example, 6 would be added 5 times if the problem were 5×6=30. The binary arithmetic involved in this example is shown below. Each number is four bits long; this should result in an eight-bit

product when the multiplication is complete.

The beginning conditions show the computer to be holding all zeros in the positions that will be occupied by the product when the multiplication problem is complete. This is a simplification—in normal computer operation, the "6" would have been held here when the instruction to "multiply by 5" was given. But the purpose of this description is to illustrate how multiplication can be done by binary addition, so we can assume a starting point of all zeros.

Five additions of "6" are then performed. Each requires a full addition process like that described earlier in this section; therefore the multiplication instructions performed by computers are among those that require the most time.

After each addition is completed, a product is formed, but the first four products in our case are incomplete. Hence they are called partial products. This is the term most commonly used in computers.

Division

It should be clear to the reader that computers perform all the basic arithmetic operations described up to now by reducing the operation to one of binary addition. The same is true of division.

Division is done by successive subtractions of the divisor from the dividend and remainder. We have explained earlier that subtraction is performed by adding a complemented subtrahend to the minuend. For the purpose of the division description, however, we will refer to the process as subtraction, thereby concentrating only on the results and not the process by which subtraction is actually accomplished.

To begin, let's review the names given to the quantities involved in a division problem: *dividend* is the number to be divided by the *divisor*, and the result is the *quotient*.

Multiplication Problem   5 x 6 = 30

Multiplicand 6 = 0 1 1 0   Multiplier 5 = 0 1 0 1

                              32   16 8 4 2 1

                    64 128

Beginning Conditions ⟶ 0 0 0 0 0 0 0 0

                        +   0 1 1 0   1st addition
                                                   6 + 0 = 6

1st Partial Product ⟶ 0 0 0 0 0 1 1 0

                        +   0 1 1 0   2nd addition
                                                   6 + 6 = 12

2nd Partial Product ⟶ 0 0 0 0 1 1 0 0

                        +   0 1 1 0   3rd addition
                                                   6 + 12 = 18

3rd Partial Product ⟶ 0 0 0 1 0 0 1 0

                        +   0 1 1 0   4th addition
                                                   6 + 18 = 24

4th Partial Product ⟶ 0 0 0 1 1 0 0 0

                        +   0 1 1 0   5th addition
                                                   6 + 24 = 30

Final Product ⟶ 0 0 0 1 1 1 1 0

In computers, the dividend is twice the length (in number of bit positions) of both the divisor and quotient. This is not to say that the dividend is twice the absolute value of the divisor and quotient, or even that its absolute value is larger than the divisor and quotient, but only that if the divisor and quotient are represented by four bit positions, then the dividend is represented by eight bit positions. In our example, we will use the four and eight bit positions.

The process involved is somewhat like the simple pencil-and-paper division process in which the reader makes a trial division of the divisor into the most significant part of the dividend. If the division is successful, a number is placed in the quotient and the reader makes a trial division of the divisor into the remainder. Again, a digit of the quotient is formed, based upon the results of the trial division, and the process is repeated. This goes on until the remainder is less than the divisor, at which time the

process is complete (unless the problem is to be carried into fractions).

The computer mechanizes this process by performing the following steps:

a. The divisor is aligned with the most significant half of the dividend. (In our example, the four-bit divisor is lined up with the four leftmost positions of the eight-bit dividend.)

b. The divisor is then subtracted from the most significant half of the dividend, and the resulting difference is examined.

c. If the difference is positive (we will assume that we are dealing only with positive numbers in the dividend and divisor for now), a one (1) is placed in the quotient. This indicates that the "trial division" was successful.

d. If the difference is negative, indicating that the "trial division" was unsuccessful and that an "overdraw" occurred, a zero (0) is placed in the quotient.

e. The next step taken depends upon Steps c and d above. An "overdraw" requires that the dividend be restored to its original value, just as it must be done mentally in pencil-and-paper division. This is accomplished simply by adding the divisor to the dividend, thus eliminating the results of the subtraction.

f. Regardless of whether the difference in the first subtraction was positive or negative, the computer must move on to the next position. It does so by shifting the divisor one position to the right with respect to the dividend, just as is done in pencil-and-paper division. At this point we are actually dealing with the remainder (assuming a successful first "trial division"), so we will now call what is left of the dividend the "remainder" for the rest of this description.

g. The second subtraction of the divisor—from the remainder in this case—is then done, and the difference is examined. A positive difference causes a one (1) to be placed in the quotient, and a negative difference results in a zero (0) in the quotient. If made necessary by a negative difference, the value of the remainder is restored by adding the divisor back to eliminate the results of an unsuccessful "trial division."

h. The process of subtracting, forming a quotient bit, and shifting the divisor to the right is then performed two more times for our example. A total of four subtractions, three shifts, and four quotient bits are required for an eight-bit dividend and four-bit divisor.

At this point, a four-bit quotient has been formed and the dividend has ceased to exist. A four-bit remainder, which of course is all 0s in the case of an even division, does exist, however. So the results of our computer division are a four-bit quotient and a four-bit remainder after an eight-bit dividend has been divided by a four-bit divisor.

It should be obvious to the reader that the process of adding back the divisor to the dividend (remainder) after a "trial division" will reduce the speed at which a computer can perform division problems. This process is called "the restoring method of division." It is not used in any modern machine.

A more sophisticated process, based upon sign changes in the dividend (remainder), is now used. This process eliminates the "add back," and naturally it is called the "nonrestoring process." To illustrate: Assume that the divisor and dividend are both positive numbers. If the difference is negative, an overdraw occurred, a 0 can be placed in the quotient, and the divisor can be shifted with respect to the remainder. The difference referred to throughout this discussion is actually the remainder, so the sign of the remainder is now negative. Now the divisor is *added to* the remainder, not subtracted. If the sign of the difference stayed negative, the "trial division" was successful and a 1 can be placed in the quotient. If the sign of the difference (remainder) changed again, negative to positive this time, however, it indicates that the "trial division" was unsuccessful and a 0 must be placed in the quotient.

So in the nonrestoring method of division, a sign change in the remainder indicates an overdraw and reverses the process (from subtraction to addition and vice versa) performed between the divisor and remainder. An overdraw places a 0 in the quotient, while no overdraw places a 1 in the quotient.

Floating-point Arithmetic

The previous sections dealing with binary arithmetic used only four-bit numbers without regard to whether they were positive or negative or whether they were integers, fractions, or a combination. Of course, computers must know these things in order to make the results meaningful.

First to be discussed are the positive and negative signs. Most machines use one bit position of each number as the sign; a 0 usually indicates a positive number, and a 1 usually indicates a negative number. Computer arithmetic using signed numbers follows the same rules as the pencil-and-paper arithmetic with which the reader is familiar.

Next to be considered is the placement of the decimal point, the "binary point" in this case, but for the purposes of this discussion "decimal point" will serve. There are two basic ways in which the decimal point is handled by computers. They are:

a. Fixed point, in which the decimal-point position is established by the basic computer design.
b. Floating point, in which the position of the decimal point in each number is indicated by a portion of the number set aside for that purpose.

Each of the above has advantages and disadvantages. Fixed-point arithmetic simplifies design of the computer and is fast, but it imposes a burden on the programmer. All numbers entered into the machine and all the results of the calculation must be "scaled" by the programmer so that they have meaning.

Two common placements of a fixed point are:

a. To the far right, so that all numbers are to the left. This machine is called an integer or character machine because it can handle only whole numbers or characters that do not use decimal points.
b. To the far left, between the sign position and the most significant position of the number. All computers with such an arrangement would be called fractional machines because all numbers handled would be less than 1.

Floating-point machines, on the other hand, relieve the programmer of the burden of "scaling," but the design is more complex, and the completion of the arithmetic is slower. It was mentioned earlier that a portion of each number in a floating-point machine is set aside to indicate the position of the decimal point. The number of positions is established by machine design. Let's use a typical example of a machine that has a thirty-two-bit number and a sign position, like the format shown in Figure 3(A).

The small arrows indicate the possible positions that the decimal point could occupy in this number; ranging from the far right to the far left there are thirty-three positions. In this case, there must be added to the number a section capable of counting to thirty-two. This would require six positions, as shown in Figure 3(B).

The name given to the section assigned to hold the position of the decimal point varies. Some call it the exponent—it is effectively the power to which the number is raised—while others call it the "characteristic." Point position indicator is a simple name used for the rest of this discussion.

The point position indicator in our example has six bit positions and, of course, is capable of counting higher than thirty-two but is not required to do so in our application. Note that this indicator is part of all data and as such it must accompany the number everywhere. It would thus extend the format of each number as shown in Figure 3(C).

The point indicator in our case is simply a count of how many positions are to the right of the point. When a number is brought into the arithmetic unit to be operated upon by another number, the counts in their respective point position indicators must be equal for the results to be meaningful. Therefore, the arithmetic unit shifts one or both of the numbers until the counts are equal. Assume that two short numbers are to be added as shown in (D) in the figure. Until the decimal points are aligned, the results would be meaningless.

The first number in Figure 3(D) is $17.50; an arrow indicates the position of the point. Shown next in Figure 3(D) is a

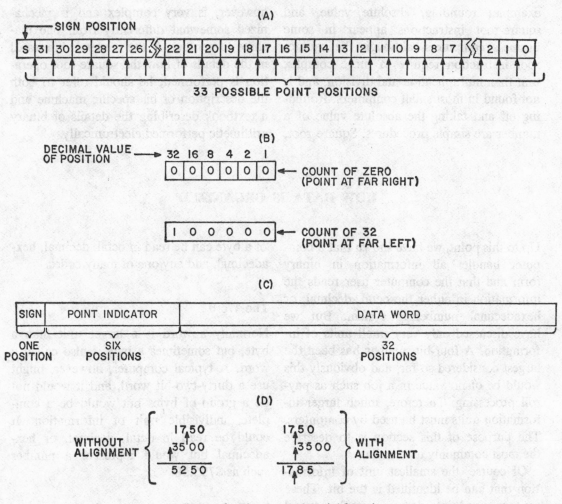

Figure 3. Floating-point Arithmetic

number equal to .35 ($.35); again, the arrow indicates the position of the point. If these two numbers were added in their current positions, the result would be a meaningless 5250. Therefore, in the floating-point machine, the numbers are shifted until the arrows are aligned. (The arrows represent the point indicator.) Addition is then performed. The result this time is 1785, and the point indicator of the $17.85 result is set to 2, indicating two positions to the right of the point.

Special Arithmetic Operations

Throughout this book we will concentrate on the principles of general-purpose com-

puters, not the machines designed to handle higher mathematics and scientific problems. To illustrate the difference: A machine designed for general-purpose use most likely would not have the trigonometric functions "built in" to its structure. These functions could be performed by the general-purpose machine but only after the user had broken them down into steps that could be performed by that machine. For example, one scientific function might require twenty-five or more steps in a general-purpose computer.

In addition to the add, subtract, multiply, and divide operations that a general-purpose computer can perform, there are a few others that the reader may encounter. For example: rounding, absolute value, and square-root instructions appear in some business computers, although the square-root instruction requires a more complex unit than multiplication and division, and is not found in most small computers. Rounding off and taking the absolute value of a number are simple procedures. Square root, however, is very complex and is mechanized somewhat differently from one machine to another. If the reader is interested in the details of how the square-root operation is performed, he should refer to both the description of his specific machine and a textbook describing the details of binary arithmetic performed electronically.

HOW DATA IS ORGANIZED

Up to this point, we have shown that a computer handles all information in binary form and that the computer user reads the information in either the octal, decimal, or hexadecimal numbering system. But we have discussed only very small units of information. A four-bit number has been the largest considered so far, and obviously this would be of no value in a job such as payroll processing. Therefore, much larger information units must be used by computers. The purpose of this section is to describe the most commonly used units.

Of course, the smallest unit of information that can be identified is the bit. These are organized into larger units in several ways, and the first of these is the byte.

The Byte

This unit of information, which was introduced to the data-processing industry sometime in the 1950s, is a group of eight bits handled as a unit. This is not to say that several bytes cannot be placed end to end and considered as a larger unit of information—they can be, and often are.

A group of eight positions was chosen as a unit of information because this many positions offer 256 combinations and thus have the ability to represent many characters. When character codes are discussed later in this book, the value of the byte will become evident. Of course, binary contents of a byte can be read in octal, decimal, hexadecimal, and any one of many codes.

The Word

Normally a word is a larger unit than a byte, but sometimes a byte is also called a word. A typical computer, however, might use a thirty-two-bit word, and it would not be a group of bytes but would be a complete, indivisible unit of information. It could be read in octal, decimal, or hexadecimal but would represent a number such as $795.50.

The Record

When a group of data consisting of many bytes or words is handled as a unit of information and moved from one storage medium to another, the group is usually called a record. There is no standard record size in the data-processing industry. The size is usually based on intended application. For example, the history of a single sale at an electronic cash register may consist of 256 bytes and be considered a record. On the larger computers, a record may consist of thousands of words.

The File

The word "file" means a group of records, although there is no standardization in the number of records in a file. A file is usually named for the kind of information it holds. Special marks (binary, of course) are usually placed between files in the storage medium.

A Volume

A volume is usually a group of files, but there is no industry standard. Most people use "volume" to mean a large physical division of storage, such as a reel of magnetic tape or a disk pack.

Numbering of Bit Positions

Up to now, we have numbered bit positions by the decimal value they represent, in order to illustrate how numbering systems and binary arithmetic work. This is not the way in which bit positions are normally labeled, but it has a direct relationship.

In the example below, a byte is shown with the bit positions labeled 0 through 7; the respective decimal values are shown above.

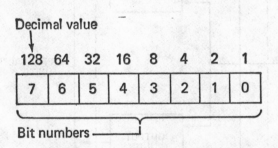

Without going into a detailed explanation, it can be stated that the bit number represents a power of 2. For example, the bit number can be considered an exponent like the "square" or "cube" of a decimal number. Bit position 2 is the "square" of a 2, and bit position 3 is the "cube" of a 2. "Two" is the base of the binary numbering system, so the byte shown above could really be shown as follows:

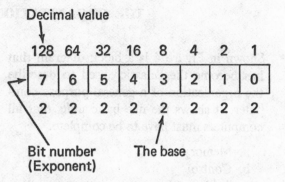

The advantage of numbering bit positions in this fashion is that the decimal value of a given bit position can be determined directly from the bit number. Bit 4, for example, is a "2" raised to the fourth power. The reader can then quickly do the mental arithmetic ($2 \times 2 \times 2 \times 2$) to arrive at the decimal value of bit 4 to be 16. A disadvantage, of course, is that most people are not accustomed to starting to count at 0.

Treating 0 as a number is a concept with which the reader must become familiar. It was mentioned in the description of the byte that eight bits could assume 256 combinations. The lowest number in these 256 combinations is 0, all eight bits being 0s, and the highest number is 255, all eight bits being 1s. This is how 256 combinations are produced.

Other Data Divisions

Characters, messages, and blocks are also terms used to describe data divisions. They do not have a fixed definition but are generally accepted to mean the following.

a. Character—a small group of bits (four to eight) holding a code representing a character such as A, ¢, 9, etc.
b. Message—usually a group of bytes, words, or characters, possibly even several records, sent between two locations.
c. Block—a group of data handled as a unit, most often a group of bytes, words, or characters.

THE ORGANIZATION OF A COMPUTER

Shown in Figure 4 is a block diagram that has become the "classic" used to describe the organization of a general-purpose computer. It shows the five basic units that all computers must have to be complete:

a. Memory
b. Control
c. Arithmetic
d. Input
e. Output

The broken lines show the organization of modern machines. Arithmetic and control units have become combined and called the processor, while the input and output units have also been combined and internal control capability added to lessen their dependence upon the control unit. They are now commonly called the input-output controller.

Memory

The memory has the most clear-cut function; it stores both the instructions that the computer executes and the data to be used. Of course, the memory also stores the results when computations are completed. Memories provide only temporary storage, however. They are usually loaded with instructions, called the program, when the computer is made ready for use, and the program acquires the information to be operated on. The program, data to be operated on, and the results are usually held in a permanent storage medium such as punched cards, magnetic tape, or magnetic disks. When power is turned off at the computer, the information held in the memory is lost.

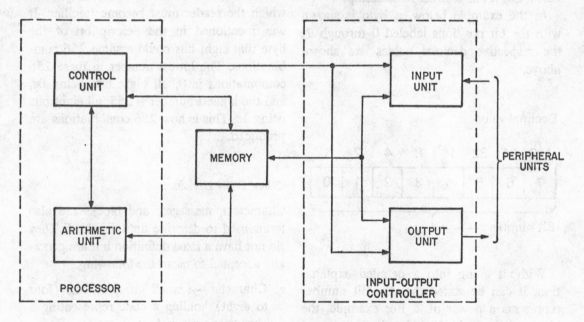

Figure 4. Block Diagram of a Typical Computer

Arithmetic Unit

Binary arithmetic, the logical operations mentioned earlier, and some special func-

tions are performed by the arithmetic unit. The primary components of the arithmetic unit are banks of bi-stable devices, which are called registers. Their purpose is to hold the numbers involved in the calculation and to temporarily hold the results until they can be transferred to memory. At the core of the arithmetic unit is a very high-speed binary adder, which performs at least the four basic arithmetic functions (addition, subtraction, multiplication, and division). Typical modern computers can perform as many as one hundred thousand additions of two, thirty-two-bit binary numbers within a second.

Control Unit

Four of the basic units operate only in response to commands from another unit: the control unit. This unit is started when power is applied to the machine, and it carries out the operations necessary to acquire some instructions and place them in memory. The user then determines what the computer will do by providing the program from permanent storage and notifying the control unit that the program is available. This might require the user to push a button labeled "load from disk." The control unit responds by acquiring the program, storing it in memory, and then reading it from memory one instruction at a time and taking the action called for by the instruction.

Typical components of a control unit are:

a. A counter that chooses the instructions, one at a time, from memory.
b. A register that holds the instructions read from memory while the instruction is being executed.
c. A decoder that takes the coded instruction and breaks it down into the individual commands necessary to carry it out.
d. A clock, which while not a clock in the sense of a timekeeping unit, does produce marks at regular intervals. Of course, these timing marks are electronic and very rapid.

Input/Output Units

The input and output units, as their names imply, move information and programs into the computer and the results of computations out of the computer. In all modern machines, the data are moved between memory and the peripheral devices. Commands from the control unit choose the input or output unit and the peripheral device with which data are to be exchanged, and the control unit chooses the area in memory from which data are to be moved or into which data are to be transferred.

The input and output units co-ordinate the data exchange with the peripheral devices. Invariably, the computer is much faster than the peripheral devices, so the I/O units must temporarily store information and synchronize the data transfer.

Recent Developments

As integrated circuits have become cheaper and more powerful, the input/output units have evolved into very powerful data-processing devices in themselves, operating nearly independently, with only minimum control from the control unit. In addition, the I/O units have become subdivided into groups dealing with specific devices. For example, one I/O unit is provided for displays and keyboards, another for magnetic disks, another for magnetic tapes, and another for printers.

A common arrangement in use today is shown in Figure 5. In such an arrangement, the control unit chooses one or more of the controllers (usually by a prearranged number), specifies whether an input or output is required, chooses the area of memory involved, and then allows the controllers to operate freely. After the controller has carried out the data exchange called for, it signals the control unit and thus the control unit knows that the operation has been completed.

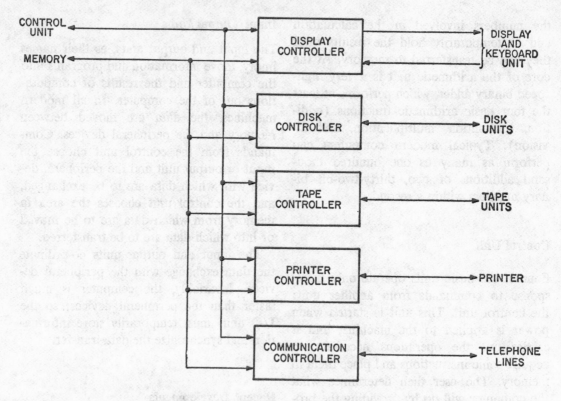

Figure 5. A Modern Input/Output Controller

MAGNETIC TAPE UNITS

Nearly everyone has used home or portable tape recorders, so the mechanism of the tape machine is widely known. It consists of a supply reel, a take-up reel, recording and reading heads, and usually some form of speed regulator. Of course, there are controls by which the tape can be started, stopped, rewound, and information either recorded or played back. All these components appear in the tape units used in the data-processing industry, and these machines differ from the home recorders primarily in size and quality.

Magnetic Recording Techniques

It is not the intention of this book to delve into the electronic circuits used in tape units or other peripheral units, but the prin-

ciples involved in magnetic recording are so important that the reader should have some knowledge of them. Hence, the following simplified description.

Most readers will recall that when electric current flows through a wire it produces a magnetic field around the wire. The polarization, or direction, of that field is determined by the direction of current flow. Of course, the strength of the field is determined by the amount of current flowing.

The reverse of this principle is that when a wire is moved through an existing magnetic field—a permanent magnet, for example—the action produces current flow in the wire. Direction of current is determined by the direction of the magnetic field, and strength of the current is determined by both the strength of the field and the speed with which the wire is moving through it.

Building on these principles, we can explain the magnetic recording and playback of binary information. First we have the recording medium—magnetic tape, in our case. Made up of a plastic base coated with magnetic material, magnetic tape is capable of being magnetized and retaining that magnetization a very long time.

Next we have the recording and reading heads. These are the "wires" referred to in the preceding description of principles. Assume that they are separate heads for the purposes of this discussion. A recording head is capable of producing a small magnetic field when current is passed through it. The field direction is reversed when the direction of current is reversed; thus the two binary digits (1 and 0) are easily represented by changes in direction of current.

There is a small gap in the recording head and, when the magnetic tape passes under this gap, the magnetic field produced by the head comes in contact with the magnetic coating on the tape. This magnetizes a small spot in the coating, in effect leaving a tiny permanent magnet.

When a tape is to be read (played back), the reading heads are used and the recording heads are inactive. Since the tape is moving we now have the situation in which a series of tiny magnetic fields is being moved rapidly past a wire, which is the reading head. As each field comes in contact with the head, it produces an electric current in the head. The direction of the current depends upon the direction of the field, which was determined by whether a 1 or a 0 was originally recorded. Thus the original binary information is read back.

So far we have covered the basic theory of recording binary information. In practice there are many variations and refinements. We will discuss what is probably the most commonly used recording technique to illustrate the possibilities. That technique is called the NRZ (nonreturn to zero), change on 1s, method. In this case, the recording head produces a magnetic field whose direction is reversed only when a 1 is to be recorded and whose direction remains unchanged when 0s are being recorded. So the direction of the field does not carry the information, but a *change* or *lack of change* in direction does.

The Tape Itself

The most commonly used data-recording tape is about a half inch wide and very thin. It has a plastic base, coated on one side with iron oxide which by being magnetized is the recording medium.

Binary digits are recorded in extremely dense patterns, the measure of which is usually expressed in bits per inch. There are several standard densities used. For example, an eight hundred bits-per-inch tape could be used on the tape units of several different manufacturers, provided that the users adhered to the basic format conventions.

Although there are many kinds of tape units in use, we can choose one as a typical example. This unit records bytes across the tape at eight hundred bits per inch in the format shown in Figures 6 and 7.

The data on this tape are organized into records, with a gap of nonmagnetized area, perhaps an inch long, between records. Interrecord gaps, as these areas are called, are where the tape comes to rest under the head when it stops, and where the tape starts again. Records are then organized into files, with a special file mark character written at the end of each file. There are also some special characters used to check that the data were recorded and read correctly, but these special characters are the subject of another discussion.

The rows in which the data is recorded are usually called tracks or channels. For example, the tape shown above has nine

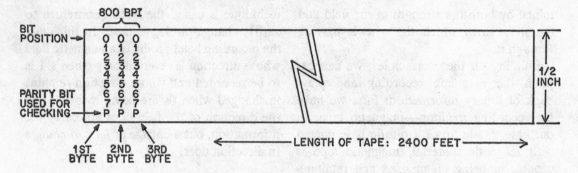

Figure 6. Tape Format Showing Bytes Recorded on Tape

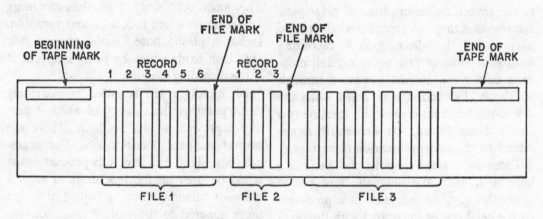

Figure 7. Organization of Records and Files on Tape

tracks, one for bit 0 of all bytes, the second for bit 1 of all bytes, etc.

The overall format of a large tape is shown in Figure 7. The beginning and end of tape marks that appear in the figure are normally adhesive strips with a reflective coating. They point out the ends of the physical tape to the control circuits in the tape drive so that recording is done within the specified area and the tape is not driven off the reels. Five to ten feet is the average tape length between the BOT mark and the end; this is called the "leader." Ten feet or more are often left between the EOT mark and the end so that records can be finished if necessary. This area is called the "trailer."

Tape Drives

Commercial tape drives use very high-quality motors, speed controls, and precision parts, but these perform the same function as those in the home tape recorder. Where the data-processing tapes differ from the home recorder is that the data-processing tapes must start and stop both often and rapidly. Without special arrangements, the tape itself could not stand the strain and would break. So data-processing tape drives have tape storage loops in which slack tape is suspended between the supply and take-up reels under very little tension. This is shown in the front view of a simple tape drive that appears in Figure 8.

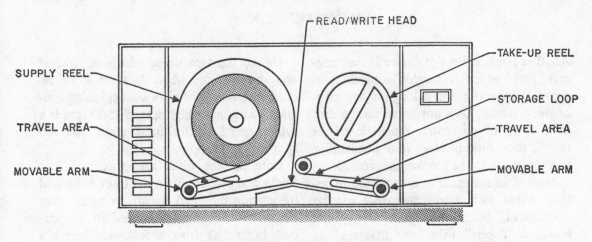

Figure 8. Front View of a Tape Unit

There are two storage loops in this tape unit, one near the take-up reel and one near the supply reel. When the tape is threaded, springs on the movable arms hold the tape, effectively storing several inches of tape in each loop under very light tension. When the tape is moved past the read/write head, tape is added to the storage loop near the take-up reel. The storage loop arm then moves past a sensor; this causes the take-up reel to turn. At the same time, tape is removed from the loop near the supply reel, the arm moves past a sensor, and the supply reel moves to restore tape to the storage loop.

Typical Instructions

Controls on the tape drive allow the operator to load and thread the tape. A typical control pushbutton would be "LOAD." After the tape is threaded, the operator pushes the load pushbutton, and the tape unit moves the tape forward until the BOT mark is under the heads. This is called the "load point." The tape is then ready to record or read.

There is also usually an on-line/off-line switch to inform the computer of the tape's readiness. On-line means ready for use, and off-line means that the computer cannot gain access to the tape.

Once the tape is prepared and on line, the computer can send instructions to the unit to manipulate the tape. Typical are:

a. Forward, with either read or write. These commands apply to one record at a time. A record is read or written and the tape drive stops with an interrecord gap at the read/write head. It should be noted that data-processing tape drives always handle one complete record at a time, so the tape always stops in an interrecord gap.

b. Fast forward. No reading or writing is done, but there are ways of sensing records or file marks passing the heads. This is a way of searching for a specific record or file.

c. Backspace. No reading or writing takes place, but the tape is moved backward by one record.

d. Rewind. Rewinds the tape to the load point.

e. Write file mark. This instruction causes the tape unit to write the mark that organizes records into files.

f. Read status. Supplies a tape status word to the computer.

The tape is usually very slow compared to the computer, so one byte at a time is exchanged between the tape and computer in synchronization with tape speed rather than computer speed. Synchronization is accomplished by the magnetic tape controller.

MAGNETIC DISKS

Another popular storage device is the magnetic disk, which is roughly equivalent in size and appearance to a long-playing phonograph record. Data are stored on the disk in a series of concentric magnetic tracks that, if they could be seen, would be similar in appearance to the grooves in a record.

Most disks are made of a very hard material, coated with a substance that can be magnetized. Within the past few years, however, "floppy" disks (or "diskettes," as they are often called) have come into widespread use. These disks are very lightweight and are made of plastic coated with a magnetic material. Their big advantages are that they can be operated by a small, inexpensive disk drive and they are relatively cheap. Because disks, whether hard or floppy, are very sensitive to contamination by dirt, they are always enclosed in some kind of a case.

A Disk Format

Shown in Figure 9 is the top view of a disk, which is often called a "platter." This example has only eight concentric tracks, although two hundred tracks or more are normal. Disks are divided into pie-shaped pieces, called sectors, and the example below shows six sectors (twenty-four is a frequently used number of sectors in the industry). The reader should be aware that the division of a disk into sectors is an electronic division, not a physical one. If a disk is examined visually, there is no indication of where sectors begin and end.

Of course, the data are recorded in binary form, magnetized in the same general scheme as the magnetic tapes described earlier. A 1 produces a magnetic pattern in one direction, and a 0 produces a pattern in the opposite direction. The data are recorded and read by the single read-and-write head shown in Figure 9.

Unlike the tape units, which are started and stopped only when data are to be recorded or read, disks are kept spinning constantly at a fairly high speed; 1500 rpm is a typical speed for the "hard" disks, and 360 rpm for the "floppys."

Data on the disks are organized into tracks and sectors. First, the track is located by moving the head toward or away from the center. Sectors are located by the circuits in the disk drive, as follows: There is a series of magnetic marks around the disk that designate the beginning of each sector. A counter in the disk drive uses these marks to keep track of which sector is under the read/write head. Thus the section of the disk in which data are to be recorded or read is chosen by track and sector number.

There are several ways in which the disk sectors are organized. A simple method that serves to illustrate the principles involved is as follows: Beginning in the first sector of the first track, numbers are assigned to each section. In the example disk in Figure 9, the first number would be track 1, sector 1. This would proceed through track 8, sector 6, and result in the series of numbers shown below:

11	31	51	71
12	32	52	72
13	33	53	73
14	34	54	74
15	35	55	75
16	36	56	76
21	41	61	81
22	42	62	82
23	43	63	83
24	44	64	84
25	45	65	85
26	46	66	86

Thus there would be forty-eight separate sections that could be chosen by the combination of a track number and a sector count. Most often, these forty-eight sections

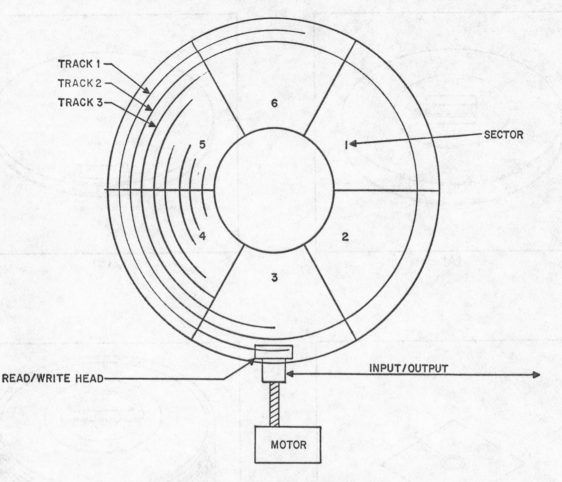

Figure 9. Top View of a Disk Format

are called "sectors," which confuses the terms somewhat but which is widely accepted. So the sample disk shown would be said to have forty-eight sectors on its top surface.

Both the top and bottom surfaces are used to record data, and the sector-numbering scheme continues on the bottom of the disk. It is necessary, however, for the circuits in the disk drive to switch to use the bottom head in order to use the lower surface of the disk.

Types of Disk Drives and Disk Packs

The simplest disk drive uses a single, nonremovable platter driven by a motor. However, this prevents the disks from being changed easily to accommodate different types of data.

A more desirable disk drive is one in which disks can easily be changed. There are three general types, which are shown in Figure 10 and listed below:

a. Top-loading, single-platter pack. In this case, the top of the disk drive opens, and the pack is placed in the drive. A pack of this type is shown in Section (A) of the figure.

b. Front-loading, single platter. The front of the drive opens, allowing insertion of an enclosed platter. The platter is then pushed down to engage the drive mechanism. (Most diskettes are this style.) Section (B) of the figure shows a "hard"

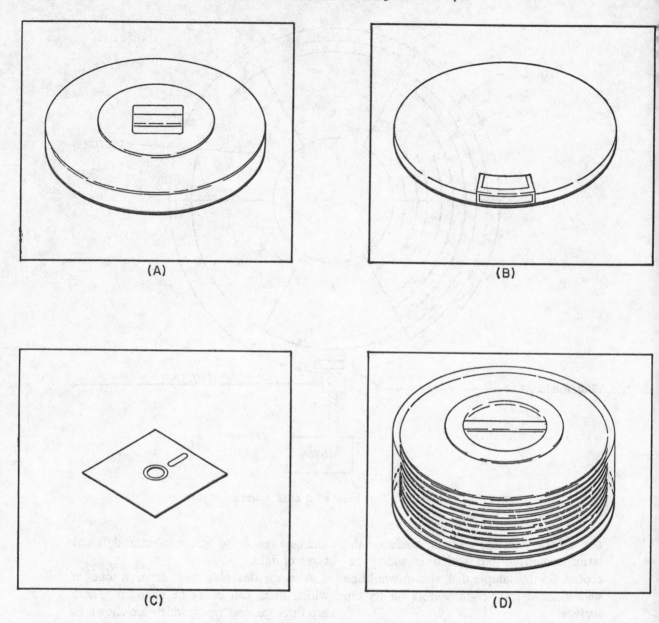

Figure 10. Three Types of Disk Packs and a Diskette

disk pack of the front-loading type, and Section (C) shows a diskette.

c. Top-loading, multiple platters. For very large storage capacity, several platters are handled and enclosed as a unit. Section (D) of Figure 10 shows a pack of this type.

Organization of the Data in a Sector

Recording density and data organization vary greatly from one manufacturer to the next. The following description, therefore, is given as a representative example.

Assume that the data is organized into bytes and that bytes are handled in blocks

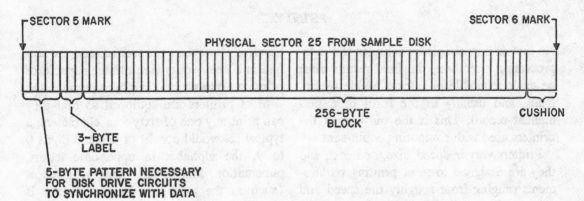

Figure 11. Layout of a Disk Sector

of 256 each. In this case, the contents of a sector would appear as shown in Figure 11. This section represents Sector 25 from the sample disk described above.

The read/write head is moved to track 2 in response to a command from a disk controller. The sector count is then checked as the disk spins. When Sector 5 is reached, the disk drive read/write circuits start handling the contents of Sector 25. Notice that the sector number "25" is a combination of track number 2 and sector number 5.

A five-byte pattern is provided so that the circuits can synchronize their operation with the disk movement. Next a three-byte label appears. This could be used to identify this sector by number or to label its contents. Then the actual data block is reached.

Each sector is often physically larger than that actually required to record the data. Called a cushion in the example, this allows for minor variations in disk speed without affecting the data processing.

A Disk Predecessor: The Magnetic Drum

A forerunner of the disk was the magnetic drum, a large, heavy cylinder, coated with magnetic material. The major disadvantages when compared with a disk were size, weight, and cost.

Data was recorded in a variety of ways, including placing registers of storage across the drum, as shown in Figure 12. This required a row of heads along the same line. It did offer the advantage, however, of reading the data in parallel rather than in the serial form that disks provide.

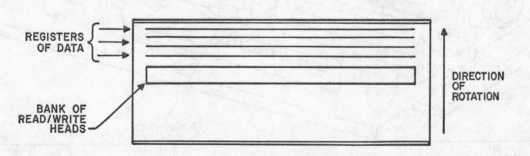

Figure 12. Sketch of a Magnetic Drum

PRINTERS

No matter how simple or complex the data-processing operation, the final results must be made available in a form usable by humans, and usually in the form of a permanent record. This is the purpose of the printers used with computing equipment.

Printers vary in speed, size, and cost, and they are designed to meet printing requirements ranging from roughly the speed and volume of a typewriter up to thousands of lines per minute. For the purpose of this discussion, however, two printers have been chosen as representative examples of those available today. The first is a lightweight matrix printer capable of printing about a hundred characters per second, and the second is a heavy-duty line printer capable of printing up to six hundred lines per minute.

Most printers are equipped so that they can print any one of sixty-four characters; a typical set would consist of decimal digits 0 to 9, the alphabet in upper-case letters, punctuation marks, and special symbols (such as the = sign). Each character is chosen by the computer when it supplies a specific code to the printer. The printer then translates the code as necessary to construct the character and imprint it on the paper being fed through the printer. Usually the printers offer variations in the char-

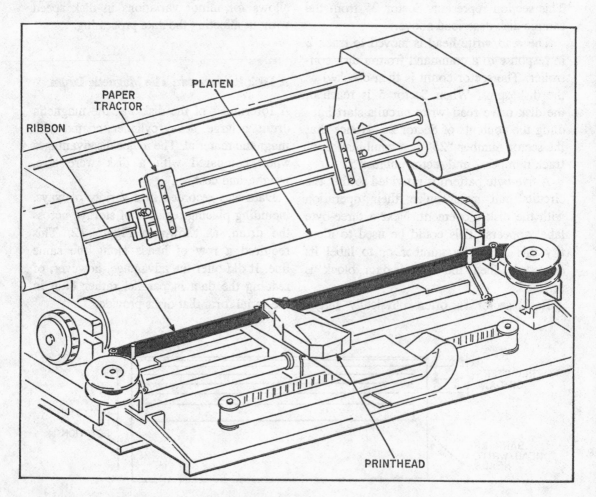

Figure 13. The Printing Mechanism of a Typical Matrix Printer

acter sets so that a given printer mechanism can easily be modified to handle special symbols or foreign languages.

Matrix Printers

The printing mechanism of the typical matrix printer chosen for this example is shown in Figure 13. A movable print head travels along a carriage, driven by a notched belt. Up to 132 character positions can be located along the carriage.

Printing is accomplished when the ends of wires are driven forward toward the platen. They make contact with the ribbon and deposit ink on the paper in a series of dots. These printers are called matrix printers because the print head wires print in a matrix pattern, seven by seven positions in our representative example. In a seven by seven matrix, there would be seven wires arranged vertically in the print head, as shown in Figure 14. Circuits in the printer then cause the print head to print columns of dots so as to form characters like those in Figure 15. It should be noted that three columns of the seven by seven matrix mentioned above are devoted to spaces between characters; the characters formed are seven dots high and four dots across.

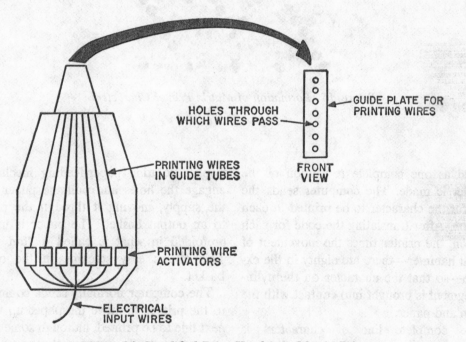

HOLES THROUGH WHICH WIRES PASS

GUIDE PLATE FOR PRINTING WIRES

FRONT VIEW

PRINTING WIRES IN GUIDE TUBES

PRINTING WIRE ACTIVATORS

ELECTRICAL INPUT WIRES

Figure 14. Simplified Print Head in a Matrix Printer

Line Printers

The printing mechanism in line printers is completely different from matrix printers. In the line printer chosen for this example the character set to be printed is on a cylinder, like that shown in Figure 16. Each segment of the cylinder (there are eighty in the example) has the full set of characters in raised form around its edge. All segments are aligned with one another—that is, all the "A's," for example, are in line.

Whenever the printer is in the print mode, the cylinder is rotating and each character in the set passes by the line to be

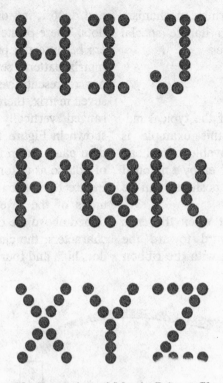

Figure 15. Formation of Matrix Printer Characters

printed as one complete revolution of the cylinder is made. The computer sends the code for the character to be printed in each position. After translating the code for each position, the printer times the movement of a print hammer—there are eighty in the example—so that the character on the cylinder segment is brought into contact with the ribbon and paper.

One complete line of characters is printed during one revolution of the cylinder. It is interesting to note that all the "A's" used in the line are printed first, then all the "B's," and so forth until finally all the letters that make up the words have been printed and the line is complete.

Paper Movement

In order to provide precise control of paper movement, printers use paper with holes punched along both edges. Pins protruding from a rotating paper-feeding mechanism engage the holes and pull the paper from the supply, moving it through the printer to an output basket. The paper is usually prefolded in what is called a "fan fold." This allows easy stacking in the output basket.

The computer normally sends commands to the printer to move the paper up to the next line to be printed, although some printers automatically advance the paper after printing a line. Most printers also include a unit that provides some automatic control of paper movement; this unit is called the vertical format unit (VFU). Mounted inside the VFU is a circular paper tape, usually with several channels of prepunched holes. This tape is driven in synchronization with the paper movement, so its position reflects the position of the print head with respect to the paper in the printer.

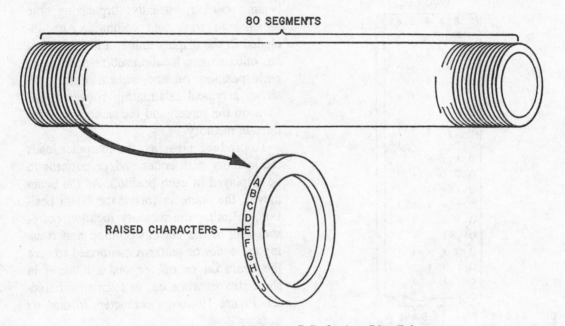

Figure 16. Typical Printing Cylinder in a Line Printer

The paper is divided into pages and subdivided into lines, and the line numbers correspond to punch positions in the VFU tape. Circuits are provided in the printer so that the computer can order the printer to sense a certain channel in the tape and move the paper until a punched hole in the tape is found.

A typical VFU tape is shown in Figure 17. If the computer gave a "top of form" command in this case, the VFU would sense for holes in Channel 7 and keep moving paper until it found one. Then the paper would be stopped, and the first line to be printed would be under the print head.

OTHER PERIPHERAL UNITS

This description deals with the remaining computer peripheral units that are considered to be of general interest. Included are operator displays and keyboards, card readers, and card punches.

Display Units

As central computers became faster and more powerful, it was possible to establish many remote display stations from which operators could all use the same computer to display information and enter data. Later, even the small machines were equipped with a fairly large display screen and keyboard oriented toward use by a person with limited training rather than a highly skilled computer operator.

The display and keyboard is usually treated by the computer just as if it were a

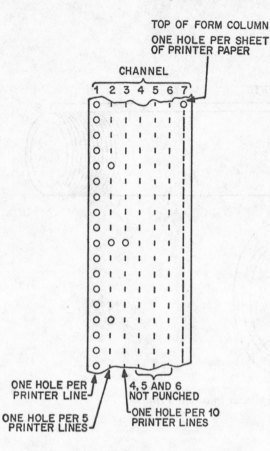

Figure 17. A Section of a Vertical-format Control Tape

are formed by dots or short strokes of the beam.

Counters are used to keep track of the beam position, usually organizing the screen into rows and columns. Also included in the display unit is a memory that has one or more locations corresponding to each position on the screen. Figure 18 shows a typical relationship between positions on the screen and the associated locations in memory.

To produce a display, the computer loads the memory with codes and/or patterns to be displayed in each position. As the beam moves, the counters follow the beam position, selecting the memory location corresponding to the current position and causing the codes or patterns mentioned to turn the beam on or off, or make it move in short strokes while on, to form the character. Figure 19 shows characters formed by dots.

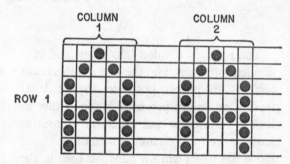

Figure 19. Characters Formed on the Display Screen

Because the picture fades very quickly, it must be repainted constantly. A TV picture is repainted thirty times a second, for example. For this reason, a memory is provided for the display, and the computer supplies only the data to be changed. If this were not done, the computer would have to send data to the display as it was repainted.

peripheral unit, such as a magnetic tape unit. That is to say, the computer usually houses display and keyboard controllers that perform the same general function as the magnetic tape controller.

Before the transfer of information between the computer and display is discussed, however, it is necessary to briefly describe the display characteristics. The screen on which information is written is simply a CRT (cathode ray tube), just like that in a television receiver. In fact, most are picture tubes purchased from the makers of TV picture tubes. In a TV receiver, a beam scans across the screen, lightening and darkening as necessary to paint a picture of many tones. Computer display units, however, have the beam either on or off, so letters, numbers, or lines

The Keyboards

The keyboards are usually closely associated with a display (although they are

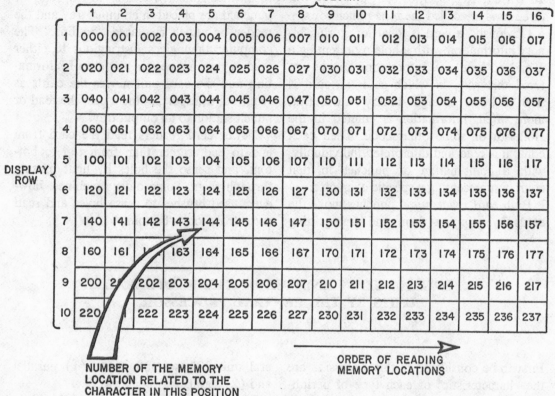

DISPLAY COLUMN

NUMBER OF THE MEMORY
LOCATION RELATED TO THE
CHARACTER IN THIS POSITION

ORDER OF READING
MEMORY LOCATIONS

Figure 18. Organization of a Typical Display Screen

sometimes incorporated with a printer), so they are described in this section. Very old computers used a modified electric typewriter to allow the operator to enter instructions and to provide a response to the operator. Fitted under the standard keyboard was a very complex mechanical assembly that could produce a code representing each key depressed and could activate a keystroke when it received a code from the computer. Modern machines, however, use a keyboard that is nearly all electronic. Each key depression produces a code, usually five to eight bits in length, and the computer responds by displaying information on a screen like that described above. The usual arrangement of data entry is that the operator types in the material and it enters temporary storage. The information is then held there until the operator verifies that it is correct and depresses a control key.

Card Readers and Punches

Until the early 1960s, punched cards were a major storage medium for computer programs and data. Recently, however, more and more programming is being done by keying in the instructions at a display and keyboard unit rather than at a card punch, and the same holds true for data entry. The programs and data then go directly to disks or magnetic tape, eliminating cards.

The most commonly used card has rectangular punches to record data, although one major manufacturer used circular punches. (The reason for one corner of a card being cut off is so that the user has a reference point to place the cards in the machine.) The card is organized into eighty columns and twelve rows. Columns are numbered left to right, but the rows are numbered top to bottom as follows: 12, 11,

10 (or 0), 1, 2, 3, 4, 5, 6, 7, 8, 9. The top three rows are called the zone punch rows.

Obviously, a card is ideal for storing binary information, with a hole representing a 1 and no hole a 0. Information can be entered this way, in which case the card is said to be a "straight binary" card. But, more often, information is entered in the Hollerith or some other code. Then each column is read and interpreted individually, with a combination of punches in that column representing a specific character.

Both card readers and punches move the cards by gripping them and transporting them mechanically. Cards to be read or punched are placed in an input tray and the reader or punch is placed "on line." The computer then gives instructions to either read or punch a certain amount of information and the card unit moves the cards as required, transporting them past the read or punch station to an output tray.

Newer card readers read the card from end to end, rather than from top to bottom, and sense the holes by light passing through them. Some older machines, however, used brushes to sense holes and read cards from top to bottom.

ORGANIZATION AND USE OF THE PERIPHERAL UNITS BY THE CENTRAL PROCESSOR

First to be considered in this discussion are the characteristics of each type of peripheral unit, because these affect the application of the unit. A summary of the characteristics is provided below:

a. *Magnetic Tape Units*. Store very large amounts of data, but are limited by relatively low speeds and the need to gain access to records serially.
b. *Magnetic Disk Units*. Store large amounts of data, have fairly high-speed access for recording or reading.
c. *Printers*. Low-speed output devices, but they provide a permanent record.
d. *Card equipment*. Low-speed input/output devices, and much card handling is required.
e. *Displays*. A very fast output device as it appears to the computer, but an operator must read the information before acting.
f. *Keyboards*. A very slow input device as it appears to the computer, and the operator must type the inputs.

Next to be discussed are the two modes normally used to transfer information between computers and their related peripheral units. These modes are: (1) parallel and (2) serial.

Parallel means that all bits of the basic unit of information (character, byte, or word) are made available at the same time. Assume that a byte is the basic unit. In this case, all eight bits would be transferred between the computer and its peripheral unit simultaneously.

Serial means that the bits of the basic unit of information are made available only one at a time, usually the least significant bit (bit 0) first. In this case, one bit after another is sent over a single line to a peripheral unit. If a bit is missed, it is lost forever, and the unit of information must be retransmitted.

The advantages of one mode with respect to another are rather obvious:

a. The serial mode requires only a single line but is slow.
b. The parallel mode is fast but requires at least as many lines as there are bits in the basic unit of information.

Regardless of whether the serial or parallel mode of transfer is used, the computer

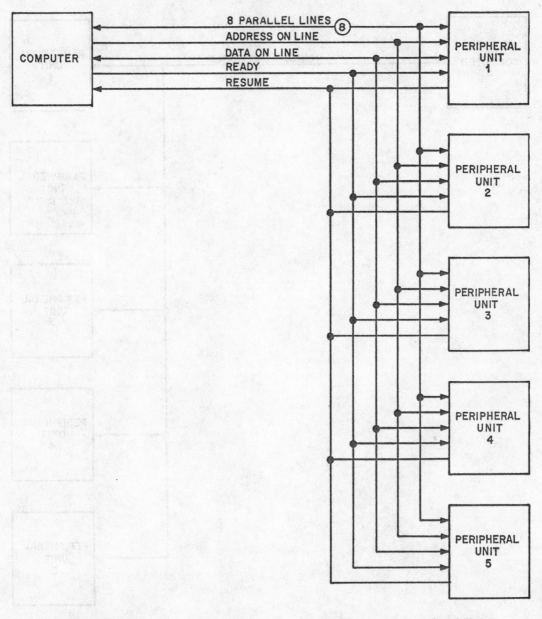

Figure 20. A Parallel Connection Between the Computer and Peripheral Units

must have some way of choosing one peripheral unit from the others. This is done by assigning an address, usually a one- or two-digit octal number, to each peripheral unit, allowing many peripheral units to be individually identified.

Shown in Figure 20 is a computer and five peripheral units connected in the parallel mode. These units are magnetic disks capable of rapid data transfer, necessitating

the parallel connection, and the connection shown is intended to transfer bytes as the basic units of information.

There are twelve lines connected between the computer and the five disk units. A data-transfer sequence to write information on a disk would be as follows:

a. The computer places address 04 on the eight parallel lines and makes the "ad-

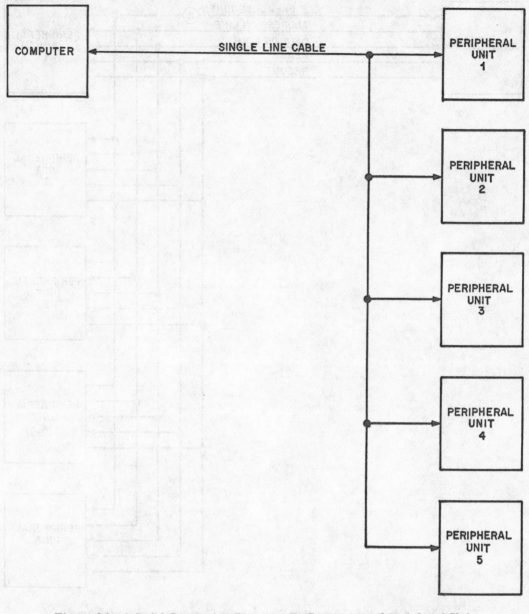

Figure 21. A Serial Connection Between the Computer and Peripheral Units

dress on line" and "ready" signals active.

b. The "address on line" signal tells all five disk units to examine the address to determine if it is their own. Only disk 04 responds with the "resume" signal.

c. The computer now recognizes that it has made contact with the desired disk, and it places the first data byte on the lines and activates the "data on line" and "ready" signals.

d. Disk 04 is the only disk that is active; hence, only this disk accepts the information and responds with a "resume" signal.

e. Each time that the computer receives the resume signal, it places the next byte on the lines. This continues until all information has been transferred and recorded on the disk.

f. Some systems use a convention by which

it is necessary to disconnect a peripheral unit when the computer is finished, but others simply cause each peripheral unit to disconnect whenever the "address on line" signal appears.

A serial connection between a computer and five peripheral units is shown in Figure 21. In this case, the data to be transferred is sent at relatively low rates. A large disk would probably not be used in this group because it can transfer data very rapidly. Typical peripheral units on this line would be printers, magnetic tape units, card equipment, and keyboards.

Since there is only a single line, the computer must place all information on the line one bit after another. A typical sequence for transferring information to the peripheral units would be as follows:

a. First, the computer shifts an "alert" byte onto the line. This special code notifies all units to clear their current status and expect a transmission.

b. Next, an address is shifted onto the line.

All units know that an address follows an "alert," so each examines the address to determine if it is its own.

c. After sending the address, the computer stops sending in order to receive a response it expects.

d. The selected unit places its own address on the line, followed by a report of its status. In turn, the computer sees that the address it received was that of the unit it selected, and it examines the status to determine that the peripheral unit is ready.

e. The computer then shifts commands and data over the line to all units, but only the selected unit uses this information.

f. In this system, disconnection of the selected unit is accomplished when the computer places the next "alert" byte on the line.

By examining the figures showing the two modes of data transfer, the reader can quickly see the major advantage of the serial mode: The connections required are very simple compared to those of the parallel mode.

QUIZ ON THE SUBJECT MATTER IN UNIT 1

1. What are the characters available in the following numbering systems?

    a.   Binary
    b.   Octal
    c.   Decimal
    d.   Hexadecimal

2. Read the following numbers in octal:
    a.   000 010 000
    b.   101 111 011
    c.   001 010 110
    d.   011 001 101
    e.   *01 000 111
    f.   *11 111 111

* When there are only two binary digits in a group, they are the "1" and "2" positions; the "4" position is the missing one.

3. Read the following numbers in decimal.

    a.   0 0 1 0 1 0 1 1
    b.   1 1 1 1 0 0 1 1
    c.   1 0 1 0 1 0 1 0
    d.   0 1 1 1 0 1 0 0
    e.   1 1 0 0 0 0 0 0

4. Count to sixteen using the binary representation.

5. Read the following numbers in hexadecimal.

     a.   1101   0000
     b.   1110   1111
     c.   0100   0101
     d.   0111   1010
     e.   0000   0111

6. Why is the binary numbering system so well suited for use in electronic computers?

7. State the rules that apply to the following basic computer elements:

     a.   OR gate
     b.   AND gate
     c.   NAND gate
     d.   NOR gate

8. Add the following four-bit binary numbers. (Do not convert to decimal.)

a.   0110   b.   1010   c.   0010
    1101   0101   1111

d.   1110   e.   1001
    0000   0011

9. Show the results of the following logical AND operations:

a.   1111   b.   1110   c.   0100
    0000   0101   0001

d.   1001   e.   1011
    1001   1100

10. Show the results of the following logical Inclusive OR operations:

a.   1010   b.   0010   c.   1000
    1101   0111   1110

d.   1001   e.   1111
    0100   0111

11. Show the results of the following logical Exclusive OR operations:

a.   0010   b.   1110   c.   0000
    1010   0011   0100

d.   1000   e.   1011
    0001   0011

12. Name the primary advantages and disadvantages of fixed-point and floating-point arithmetic.

13. How many bits are normally in a byte?

14. What are groups of records usually called?

15. Name the five basic units that make up a computer and their respective functions.

16. On magnetic tape, how is the beginning and the end of the recording area indicated?

17. What is the purpose of the interrecord gap on magnetic tape?

18. What is the purpose of the tape storage loops?

19. Define "on line" and "off line."

20. Why are magnetic disks enclosed?

21. What are the three general types of disk packs?

22. Name two general classes of printers.

23. What is the purpose of the vertical format unit on a printer?

24. There are two primary ways in which the I/O controllers can transfer data to the peripheral units: (1) serial and (2) parallel. What are the advantages and the disadvantages of each?

UNIT 2

THE COMPUTER

In this description the five basic computer units (memory, control, arithmetic, input, and output) will be opened for the reader to see inside. The essential processes performed by each unit will be explained, and the interaction among units will be discussed.

Some manufacturers of integrated circuits are already offering a "computer on a chip," so the basic computer units are inseparable and there is no way in which the chip can be repaired. A quick response to this on the part of the reader might be "I'll just throw it away when it doesn't work. Why do I need to know how it works?" Even in this case, however, the user must know what functions each unit can perform and how the units interact in order to properly apply the chip to his work.

Examples of the information that the user of a computer on a chip might require are: number of memory locations available and how they are selected, the instruction codes required to make the computer perform useful operations, and the speed with which an input/output unit can transfer data between a peripheral unit and the memory. This same information was required when the computer occupied several large cabinets, so the microminiaturization of computers has not changed the need for the user to understand what is happening inside the machine. Subjects covered in Unit 2 include those listed below. As in Unit 1, the reader will find that each section builds on previously presented material and, therefore, it is not wise to skip around when this book is being read for the first time. This unit describes the following subjects:

a. Memory organization and addressing, covering the steps involved in the use of memory by other units of the computer and factors affecting the way in which memory is organized.
b. Registers in the arithmetic unit, and their function.
c. Index registers, their purpose, organization, and examples of use.
d. The control unit, and how it decodes instructions to manipulate other elements of the computer.
e. Last, the input/output units, their organization, and how they operate.

MEMORY ADDRESSING

The term "memory" is always used to mean a storage device to which the computer has direct access. A review of the basic computer block diagram (Figure 4) shows that the memory is one of the five units of all computers and cannot be separated.

Memories have one function: *to store the computer instructions and operating data while they are in use.* Permanent storage of this information is usually provided on disks, tapes, or cards.

There are many forms of memory storage elements, ranging from the old core memories (which used small circles of magnetic material) to the "bubble" memories under development when this book was written. The most common memory elements in use today, however, are large integrated-circuit chips that store information in a great number of bi-stable circuits. These chips are placed in arrays, whose organization always depends upon the number of bits in the basic unit of information handled by the computer. If a computer was designed to handle information in bytes, then the arrays would be organized so that one byte at a time could be selected from memory. If a computer used a thirty-two-bit word, then thirty-two bits at a time could be handled by the memory.

Before proceeding with this discussion, it might be wise to review the meaning of "bi-stable." This term, as used throughout this book, means any electronic circuit capable of assuming either of two stable states and thus representing either a "1" or a "0."

Assume that the memory to be illustrated in this description is designed to handle bytes. So the memory must be organized into groups of eight bi-stables each, and the byte stored in these bi-stables must be available in its entirety. This group of eight bi-stables is called a memory location, and this location is assigned a number to distinguish it from all others. The location number is called a "memory address."

When the computer requires that information be made available to it from memory, the process is called "reading," and when the computer requires that information be stored in memory, the process is called "writing." To initiate either of these operations, the computer supplies the address to memory. It then signals the memory whether a "read" or a "write" is required. A simple diagram showing the transfer of information to and from memory appears in Figure 22.

If a read operation is called for, the memory extracts the contents of the location chosen by the address and places this information in a register from which it is available to several units in the computer. If writing is to take place, the computer

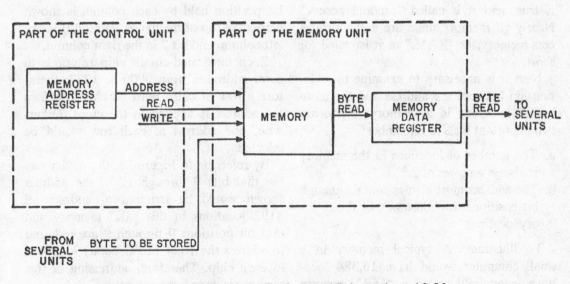

Figure 22. The Path for the Exchange of Information with Memory

supplies the address and, in addition, the byte to be stored. The most common source of information to be stored is a register called the accumulator, which is in the arithmetic unit, but information can originate at several points. In many computers, the memory unit includes a register that temporarily holds the data to be stored. This would allow an external unit to proceed with its operations after the byte was sent to the memory input register; otherwise, the external unit would have to wait until storage was completed.

A common term applied to memories is "nondestructive readout." This means that a reading operation does not change the contents of the addressed location, and the integrated-circuit memories used in modern machines are of the nondestructive readout type. Older memories, which were primarily core memories, destroyed the contents of a location when it was read. Therefore they had to temporarily hold the information read and write it back into the location from which it came.

Up to this point it has been implied that the locations in memory can be addressed in any order, with no fixed relationships existing among the previous address, the current address, and the next address. This is true, and it is called "random access." Nearly all memory units are a random-access memory, or "RAM," as it is called for short.

Next it is necessary to examine the relationship between the address and the number of locations in a memory. There are two important facts to remember:

a. The number of locations in the memory is always a power of 2.
b. The address must always contain enough bit positions to choose one of the memory locations.

To illustrate: A typical memory in a small computer would have 16,384 locations, commonly called a "16K" memory

because "K" means "kilo," or 1000. A larger machine would have a 65K memory (65,536). Relate these numbers to the bit positions required in an address shown in Figure 23.

Assume that the 16K memory must be addressed. This requires 16,384 separate combinations, or 14 bits (0 through 13). A count from 0 through 16,383 can be achieved with these positions; therefore, 14 bits are sufficient to choose each of the possible locations in a 16K memory. Projecting this to a 65K memory, Figure 23 shows that 16 bits (0 through 15) are required for addressing.

The opportunity for confusion does arise when the number of memory locations is stated in decimal, as it always is, but the address is read in octal, as it usually is. For example, a 4096-location memory would have octal addresses 0000 through 7777. The only way to avoid this confusion is to convert the address to binary and use the binary form to read octal or decimal.

The memory array of a typical desktop computer is shown in Figure 24. Each block represents an integrated-circuit chip with 1024 decimal (1777 octal) locations of one bit each. This is an "8K" memory. When 8 columns of 8 chips each are formed, this memory holds 8192 bytes. The bit position held by each column is shown across the top of the figure, with bit 0 in the left column and bit 7 in the right column.

Each integrated-circuit chip responds to octal addresses from 0000 to 1777; therefore a row of chips must be chosen before the address is applied to the chips. Otherwise, one address in each row would be selected.

By referring to Figure 23, the reader can see that bits 0 through 12 of the address shown would be required to address all 8192 locations in this "8K" memory and that bit positions 0 through 9 are required to address the 1024 (1777 octal) locations in each chip. Therefore, addressing of this memory is done in two steps:

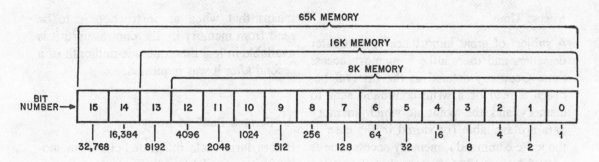

Figure 23. Typical Organization of the Memory Address

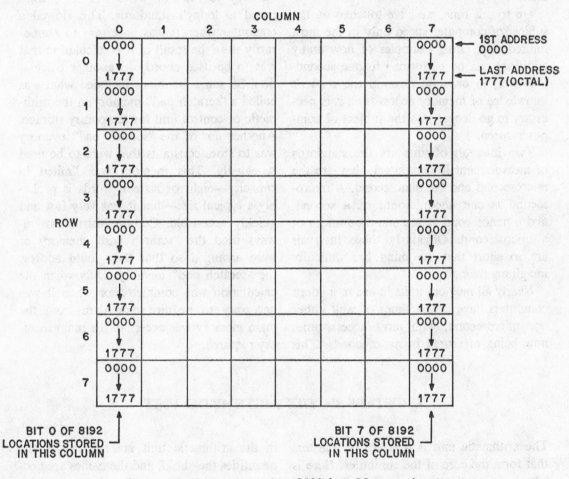

Figure 24. Organization of an 8192-byte Memory Array

a. Bit positions 10, 11, and 12 are decoded into their 8 possible combinations to choose a row.
b. Bit positions 0 through 9 are then decoded into the 1024 possible combinations to choose a location within that row.

When the selected location is reached, information is either read or written at that location and all others are left unchanged. Since this memory is a "nondestructive readout" memory, information read is also retained in the same location and does not have to be restored after having been read.

Access Time

A subject of great importance to computer designers and users alike is memory access time. Generally defined as the interval between a read or a write command sent to memory and the point at which memory data are available (or stored in the case of the write command), memory access time is one of two or three factors that determine the speed at which the computer can operate.

Up to this time, we have touched on the subject of computer speed only in the most limited way, citing examples of how many additions can be performed in one second. However, in order to develop the reader's knowledge of memory access time it is necessary to go deeper into the subject of computer speed.

Two intervals of time are the standards of measurement in computers; they are the microsecond and the nanosecond. A microsecond is one one-millionth of a second, and a nanosecond is one one-thousandth of a microsecond. Obviously these intervals are so short that the mind has difficulty imagining them.

Nearly all memory units in use in modern computers have access times of well under one microsecond, with most access times now being measured in nanoseconds. This means that when an instruction is to be read from memory by the control unit, it is available in less than one one-millionth of a second after it was requested.

A "Scratch Pad" Memory

Before large-scale integrated-circuit memories were available as the main memory unit, the time required to gain access to memory to read or write was long compared to today's standards. This slowed a computer when it was necessary to temporarily store the result of one calculation that was to be used shortly in another calculation. So some machines included what was called a "scratch pad" memory in the arithmetic or control unit for temporary storage. Another use of the "scratch pad" memory was to store constants that were to be used repeatedly. This memory was limited in capacity—eight or sixteen words is probably a typical size—but it was very fast and quickly accessible. Certain instructions always used the "scratch pad" memory or were arranged so that they could address the "scratch pad" memory. Only when the calculation was completed or when it was necessary to acquire new data from the main memory was access to the main memory required.

REGISTERS IN THE ARITHMETIC UNIT

The arithmetic unit is a group of registers that form the core of the computer. Here is where "computing" is done, and all users of data-processing equipment should have a general idea of what the components of an arithmetic unit are and how they operate together.

As most readers will recall, each of the quantities in the four basic mathematical operations has a name. It is important to review them because some of the components in the arithmetic unit are named for the quantities they hold, and the names are necessary to properly describe the flow of information among registers. Recall the following terms:

Addition—addend, augend, sum

Subtraction—minuend, subtrahend, difference

Multiplication—multiplicand, multiplier, product

Division—dividend, divisor, quotient

The first portion of this description deals with the "classic" arithmetic unit, one in which the purpose of each register is determined by the original design of the computer. The second part of the description deals with an arithmetic unit of modern design, one in which most of the registers are general-purpose in nature and the computer instructions determine how they are used.

The Classic Arithmetic Unit

A block diagram of the older unit is shown in Figure 25. Before a description is given, however, there are three facts that must be brought to the reader's attention:

a. A register is a group of bi-stables in which the number of bi-stables is usually equal to the number of bits in the basic unit of information the computer is designed to handle, although sometimes a register is a multiple of the basic unit of information.

b. The unit shown is designed to handle bytes as the basic unit of information, and No. "8" shown in circles on the diagram represents the eight bits in a byte.

c. All four of the fundamental mathematical operations $(+, -, \times, \div)$ are reduced to addtion processes by the computer.

The register of most interest is the accumulator. This register is involved in nearly all operations performed by the arithmetic unit, and it usually is the register in which the results of an operation appear.

The adder is where all of the logical operations and the addition are done, but the adder does not hold the results. They are almost immediately moved to another register, usually the accumulator.

The "A" register usually holds the second quantity involved in the operation; the accumulator usually holds the first. Because of confusion that can result in having an "A" register and an *A*ccumulator, the "A" register is called the "B" register in some computers.

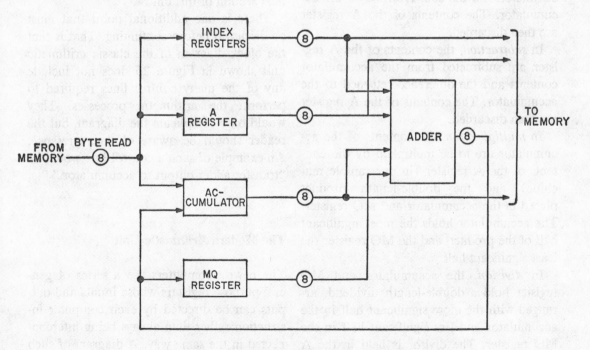

Figure 25. The Classic Arithmetic Unit

The MQ register acquired its name because it held the multiplier during multiplication and the quotient during division. Some machines have the name shortened simply to "Q" register because they hold the multiplier in the "A" register.

There are two cases in which a double-length quantity must be handled: (1) the product in multiplication is always twice the length of the basic unit of information, and (2) the dividend in division is always twice the length of the basic unit of information. These are usually handled by forming a double-length register made up of the accumulator and the MQ register.

Basic Processes

The following paragraphs briefly summarize how information is manipulated by the arithmetic unit during the four basic operations. Refer to the block diagram in Figure 25 as necessary to follow the data flow.

In *adding*, the contents of the A register are added to the current contents of the accumulator and the sum returned to the accumulator. The contents of the A register are then discarded.

In *subtraction*, the contents of the A register are subtracted from the accumulator contents and the difference returned to the accumulator. The contents of the A register are then discarded.

In *multiplication*, the contents of the accumulator are to be multiplied by the contents of the A register (in our sample machine) and the double-length product placed in the accumulator and MQ register. The accumulator holds the most significant half of the product, and the MQ register the least significant half.

In *division*, the accumulator and MQ register hold a double-length dividend, arranged with the more significant half in the accumulator and less significant half in the MQ register. The divisor is held in the A register. Division is accomplished in a number of steps equal the number of bits in the divisor. (See the description of division under Binary Arithmetic in Unit 1.) The dividend becomes progressively smaller with each step, and a partial quotient is formed with each step. The quotient is formed, one bit at a time, in the MQ register and, when the process is completed, the MQ register holds a single-length quotient and the accumulator holds a single-length remainder.

In the three *logical operations* (AND, OR, Exclusive OR), the A register holds one quantity, the accumulator the second, and the accumulator holds the results.

Often the accumulator is the only register that can be loaded directly from memory and stored directly into memory, but this varies a great deal among computers. The example shows that the A register and accumulator can be loaded from memory and that the contents of several registers can be stored in memory. Index registers shown in the block diagram are part of the arithmetic unit in some machines and part of the control unit in others. They are discussed in the next section of this unit.

There is one additional point that must be discussed before continuing. That is that the block diagram of the classic arithmetic unit shown in Figure 25 does not include any of the many control lines required to perform the arithmetic processes. They would only complicate the diagram, but the reader should be aware of their presence. An example of such a control line would be "transfer adder output to accumulator."

The Modern Arithmetic Unit

The newest computers use a series of general-purpose registers whose inputs and outputs can be directed by each computer instruction rather than always being interconnected in the same way. A diagram of such a unit appears in Figure 26.

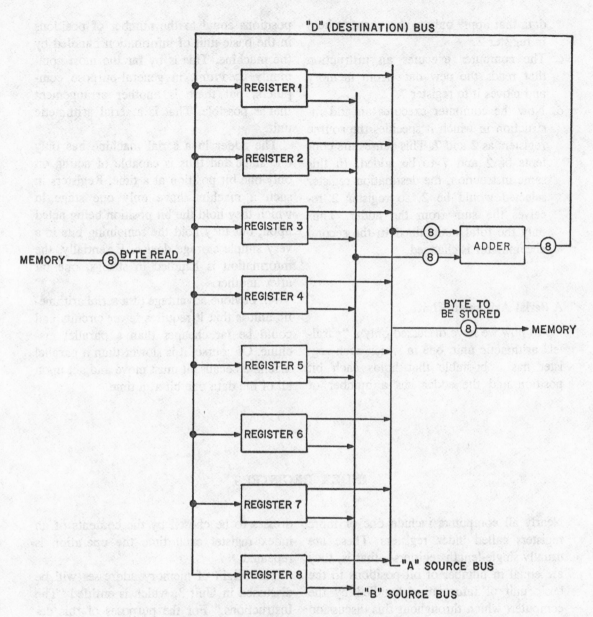

Figure 26. The Modern Arithmetic Unit

In this case, we have eight general-purpose registers and an adder. Each instruction, in addition to specifying the operation to be performed, also specifies the registers that are to be the source of the data and the register that is to be the destination of the result.

One term, "bus," used in the block diagram may be unfamiliar to the reader. In our application, it means a group of eight lines to which each of the registers can be connected.

An example of an addition operation would work in our modern unit as follows:

a. Assume that the computer program is maintaining three totals and has designated registers 1, 2, and 3 as the accumulators.

b. The computer now receives additional

data that apply only to the quantity held in register 2.

c. The computer executes an instruction that reads the new data from memory and moves it to register 7.

d. Now the computer executes an add instruction in which it specifies the source registers as 2 and 7. This causes the contents of 2 and 7 to be added. In this same instruction, the destination register selected would be 2, so register 2 receives the sum from the adder. Thus only the total maintained in the second accumulator is changed.

A Serial Arithmetic Unit

Up to now we have discussed only a "parallel" arithmetic unit, one in which each register has a bi-stable that holds each bit position and the adder has a number of positions equal to the number of positions in the basic unit of information handled by the machine. This is by far the most commonly used unit in general-purpose computers, but there is another arrangement that is possible. That is a serial arithmetic unit.

The adder in a serial machine has only one stage and thus is capable of acting on only one bit position at a time. Registers in such a machine have only one stage in which they hold the bit position being acted upon, but they hold the remaining bits in a very simple storage device. Essentially, the information is handled in strings, one bit after another.

An obvious advantage of a serial arithmetic unit is that it requires fewer circuits and could be far cheaper than a parallel machine. Of course, it is slower than a parallel machine because it must move and act upon all of the data one bit at a time.

INDEX REGISTERS

Nearly all computers include one or more registers called index registers. These are usually single-length registers—that is, they are equal in number of bit positions to the basic unit of information handled by the computer, which throughout this discussion will be assumed to be a byte.

Index registers are normally part of the arithmetic unit, but they may be included in the control unit. In some unique situations they may even be preassigned memory locations.

Regardless of where they are located, however, index registers have one primary purpose: to act as a counter for repetitive operations and modify a memory address. This allows one memory address to be chosen as the base the first time that an operation is performed, and successive addresses to be chosen by the contents of an index register each time the operation is repeated.

The origin of memory addresses will be discussed in Unit 3, which is entitled "The Instructions." For the purposes of this description, however, it is sufficient to say that they are provided as part of each instruction. The address would then follow the path shown in the block diagram in Figure 27. Although the block diagram shows a separate address adder for the purposes of a simple explanation, the main adder in the arithmetic unit is frequently used for the addition of address and index-register contents. If an index register was not to be used by the current instruction, the memory address would simply pass through the address adder unchanged.

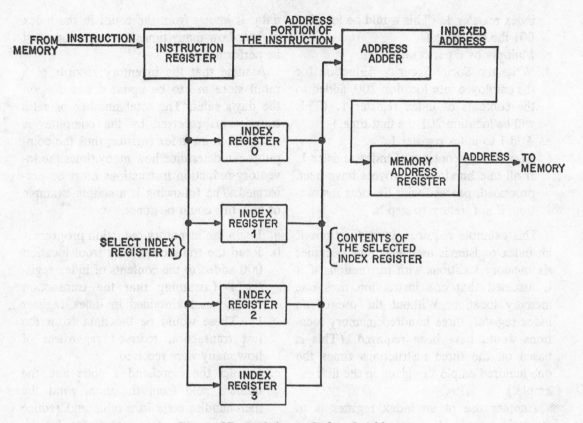

Figure 27. Path for an Indexed Address

The number of index registers used varies according to the intended use of the computer. Four are shown in the example, and this is representative of the number in a small, general-purpose computer.

It was mentioned above that an index register is used as a counter of repetitive operations. Therefore, there are usually instructions in the computer's repertoire that can load the index register with a number, step the contents up or down, store the contents of the index register in memory, read the contents of the index register back from memory, and move the contents of the index register into the accumulator, where they can be examined and tested.

The following example illustrates a simple use of an index register: Assume that there is a table of one hundred employee gross salaries stored in memory and that the Social Security tax, which is a fixed percentage of 6 per cent, is to be calculated for

each employee and stored back into another one hundred memory locations for later deduction from the gross salary. The instructions required to accomplish this would be as follows:

a. Read first employee's gross from location 001.
b. Multiply by 6 per cent.
c. Write the Social Security deduction for the first employee into location 201.

If index registers were not available, these instructions would have to be written out one hundred times, each time with different memory addresses, and this would cause the program to occupy a great deal of memory space. With the index registers available to modify addresses, however, the instructions would be written as follows:

a. Place 001 in index register 1.
b. Read the employee's gross salary from location 000 added to the contents of

index register 1. (This would be location 001 the first time.)

c. Multiply by 6 per cent.
d. Write the Social Security deduction for the employee into location 200, added to the contents of index register 1. (This will be location 201 the first time.)
e. Add 1 to index register 1.
f. Examine the contents of index register 1. If all one hundred employees have been processed, proceed with the next instruction; if not, return to step b.

This example requires six instructions if an index register is used and thus occupies six memory locations with instructions if it is assumed that one instruction uses one memory location. Without the use of an index register, three hundred memory locations would have been required. (This is based on the three instructions times the one hundred employees given in the first example.)

Another use of an index register is to maintain a count of an unknown number of data items to be processed. Assume that a number of transactions are being fed into a computer. Each time one is received, the contents of an index register are stepped up by one, so even though the total number is variable from day to day, the computer always knows exactly how many transactions have been received. At a certain point in its processing cycle, the computer is to perform operations using these transaction data. It knows from the count in the index register how many times the operation must be performed.

Assume that the inventory records of a retail store are to be updated based upon the day's sales. The total number of sales transactions received by the computer is recorded in an index register; thus the computer can determine how many times the inventory-reduction instructions must be performed. The following is a simple example of how this could be done:

a. Begin the inventory-reduction program.
b. Read the transaction data from location 000 added to the contents of index register 1 (assuming that the transaction count was maintained in index register 1). These would be the data from the last transaction received regardless of how many were received.
c. Extract the merchandise code and the number sold from the data. Find the merchandise code in a table and reduce the number of items remaining by the number sold.
d. Reduce the index-register contents by 1 and determine if it has yet reached 0.
e. If the index register is 0, all transaction data have been processed. In this case, proceed to the next job.
f. If the index register is not yet 0, read the transaction data from location 000 added to the contents of index register 1 and perform step c again.

REGISTERS IN THE CONTROL UNIT

Instructions stored in memory determine what operations the computer will perform. Collectively, the instructions are called the computer program.

Instructions are read from memory, one at a time, and moved into the control unit. There they are decoded, and the control unit produces signals that are distributed throughout the computer as necessary to carry out the instruction. Key registers in the control unit are shown in Figure 28.

A typical instruction consists of two parts: (1) an operation code that specifies what must be done, and (2) a memory address that specifies the location in memory from which data must be read and brought

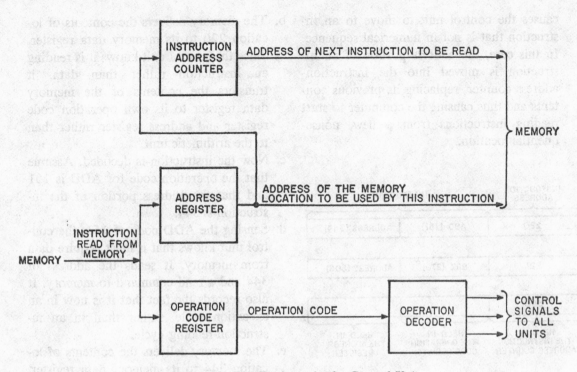

Figure 28. Key Registers in the Control Unit

to the arithmetic unit to be acted upon. Of course, the address portion of the instruction could also specify a memory location in which information from the arithmetic unit is to be stored. There are several formats in which instructions may appear, but this simple one is sufficient to illustrate operation of the control unit.

One of the things that most readers may find confusing is the difference between: (1) the address of an instruction and (2) the address portion of an instruction. To simplify:

a. Both instructions and data are stored in memory. In both cases, they are read from memory in the same way: The address of a memory location and a read signal are sent to the memory, and the memory delivers the contents of that location. The control unit knows whether the memory output is an instruction or data.

b. The address of a memory location from which an instruction is to be read is

called an instruction address. It is held by the instruction-address counter in the control unit. Instructions are normally read in sequence, so each time an instruction is executed the count is stepped up by one.

c. The address portion of an instruction is part of the instruction read from memory. It is normally delivered to the control unit and held there until the operation code is decoded and the control unit knows how the address is to be used. Then the address is sent to memory with a signal to either read or write data.

d. So the address of an instruction is called the *instruction address,* and the address portion of an instruction is called simply the *address.*

One path shown in the control-unit figure may also be confusing. That path shows the contents of the address register being sent to the input of the instruction-address counter. The reason for this is that there is an instruction called "branch," which causes the control unit to move to an instruction that is not in numerical sequence. In this case, the address portion of an instruction is moved into the instruction-address counter, replacing its previous contents and thus causing the computer to start reading instructions from a new, nonsequential location.

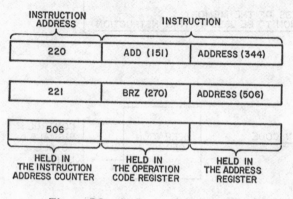

Figure 29. An Instruction Sequence

The best way to illustrate how the control unit works is to follow a sequence for a typical instruction. Assume it is ADD, which means: Acquire the contents of a specific location, move them to the "A" register in the arithmetic unit, add them to the accumulator, and place the results in the accumulator. This instruction, the format of which is shown in Figure 29, would be executed in the following manner:

a. The contents of the instruction-address counter (assume it is 220 octal) and a read command are sent to memory, and the control unit records the fact that it is in an instruction-reading cycle.

b. The memory delivers the contents of location 220 to its memory data register. Since the control unit knows it is reading an instruction rather than data, it transfers the contents of the memory data register to its own operation code register and address register rather than to the arithmetic unit.

c. Now the instruction is decoded. Assume that the operation code for ADD is 151 and that the address portion of the instruction is 344.

d. Sensing the ADD code of 151, the control unit knows that it must acquire data from memory. It sends the address of 344 and a read command to memory. It also records the fact that it is now in an execution cycle, rather than in an instruction-reading cycle.

e. The memory delivers the contents of location 344 to its memory data register. This time, however, the control unit transfers the contents of the memory data register to the A register in the arithmetic unit.

f. Continuing to hold and decode the ADD instruction, the control unit produces the signals necessary to move the contents of the A register and accumulator to the adder, add them, and return the results to the accumulator.

g. The control unit allows a certain amount of time for the operation to be completed. It then knows it is free to acquire the next instruction from memory, and it does so by stepping the instruction-address counter by 1 (to 221 in this case) and reading the next instruction from memory.

THE INPUT/OUTPUT UNITS

Up to now we have discussed the operation of the memory, arithmetic, and control units of a general-purpose computer. While the details of these units vary from one computer to the next, the basic organization of these units is similar, so the descriptions given apply in general to all machines. The input/output units, however, differ greatly from one computer to the next, so the following description is based on a representative example.

Complex I/O units are necessary because the peripheral units differ so much from one another and from the computer. The first difference to consider is speed: The computer is always much faster than the peripheral units. Another major difference is data

form: The peripheral unit nearly always requires that the data form be changed. Last, the computers are all electronic, while the peripheral units almost always have mechanical features that must be taken into consideration when they handle data. To summarize: An I/O unit must compensate for speed and data-form differences between the computer and the peripheral unit,

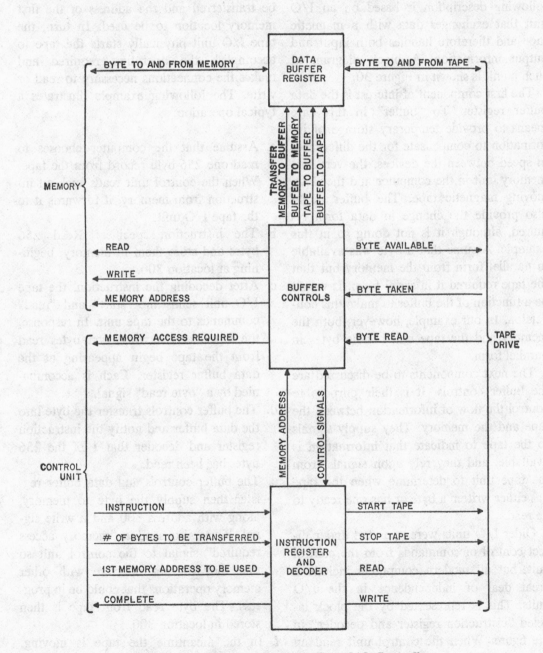

Figure 30. A Typical Magnetic Tape I/O Controller

and an I/O unit must take into account the mechanical features of the peripheral unit.

Some peripheral units only receive data from the computer; a display or a card punch is an example of such a unit. Others, such as a keyboard or card reader, only provide inputs to the computer. In order to illustrate the features that are common to both input and output units, however, the following description is based on an I/O unit that exchanges data with a magnetic tape and therefore handles both input and output information. A block diagram of such a unit is shown in Figure 30.

The first component of interest is the data buffer register. To "buffer" in this case means to provide temporary storage of information to compensate for the differences in speed between the devices, the very fast memory unit in the computer and the slow-moving magnetic tape. The buffer might also provide the change in data form required, although it is not doing so in this example. Assume that a byte was available in parallel form from the memory but that the tape required it in serial form. It would be a function of the buffer to make this conversion. In our example, however, both the memory and the tape unit handle bytes in parallel form.

The next components to be discussed are the buffer controls. It is their purpose to control the flow of information between the tape and the memory. They supply signals to the tape to indicate that information is available, and they rely upon signals from the tape unit to determine when the tape has either written a byte or has one ready to be read.

Older I/O units were operated under direct control of commands from the control unit, but all modern computers include a great deal of independence in the I/O units. This is represented by the block labeled "instruction register and decoder" in the figure. When the control unit read an instruction from memory and found it to be an I/O instruction for magnetic tape, it immediately forwarded the instruction to the tape I/O unit and proceeded with the next instruction to be executed.

The instruction sent to the tape I/O unit would choose the operation to be performed (read, write, rewind, etc.). If reading or writing was chosen, the instruction would also specify the number of bytes to be transferred and the address of the first memory location to be used. In turn, the tape I/O unit physically starts the tape to accomplish the operation required and makes the connections necessary to read or write. The following example illustrates a typical operation:

a. Assume that the computer chooses to read one 256-byte record from the tape. When the control unit reads such an instruction from memory, it forwards it to the tape I/O unit.

b. The instruction specifies: Read 256 bytes and store them in memory, beginning at location 300.

c. After decoding the instruction, the tape I/O unit sends the "start" and "read" commands to the tape unit. In response, the tape starts moving, and bytes read from the tape begin appearing at the data buffer register. Each is accompanied by a "byte read" signal.

d. The buffer controls transfer the byte into the data buffer and notify the instruction register and decoder that 1 of the 256 bytes has been read.

e. The buffer controls and data buffer register then supply the byte to memory, along with address 300 and a write signal. They also send a "memory access required" signal to the control unit so that they do not interfere with other memory operations that could be in progress. The byte read from tape is then stored in location 300.

f. In the meantime the tape is moving, slowly compared to computer speed, and the next byte is read. It is accepted and transferred to memory address 301. (The address held in the tape I/O unit is stepped up by 1 each time a byte is received.)

g. When the 256th byte is read and stored, the tape I/O unit knows that the operation is complete. (It has compared the number of bytes to be read with the number actually read throughout the entire operation.) It then sends a "stop tape" signal to the tape unit and a "complete" signal to the control unit.

h. At the tape unit, the tape stops at the gap between records, ready for the next operation.

i. In the control unit, the complete signal indicates that the 256-byte record has been read and can now be used. In addition, it means that the tape unit is finished and another I/O operation can be conducted.

QUIZ ON THE SUBJECT MATTER IN UNIT 2

1. State the primary purpose of the computer memory.

2. What information is sent to memory to begin its operation?

3. What does the term "nondestructive readout" mean?

4. How many memory locations can be addressed by a fourteen-bit address?

5. What is the highest address read in octal in:
   a. An 8K memory?
   b. A 16K memory?

6. State the purpose of the arithmetic unit.

7. State the purpose of the accumulator.

8. What does the name MQ register mean?

9. Define "double length."

10. What is the most important advantage of using general-purpose registers in an arithmetic unit?

11. Describe the purpose of index registers.

12. What is the most important advantage of using index registers?

13. State the primary purpose of the control unit.

14. What are the two basic parts of an instruction?

15. What is the purpose of the instruction-address counter?

16. What is the operation called that replaces the contents of the instruction-address counter with a new, nonsequential memory address?

17. What is the relationship between the computer and the peripheral units with regard to the rate at which they can handle data?

18. A very important component of the input-output controllers is the data buffer. Describe its purpose.

19. What is the most important advantage of the independent I/O controller?

20. What is the purpose of the buffer controls shown in the block diagram of the tape input-output controller?

UNIT 3

THE INSTRUCTIONS

When a computer is being designed, one of the first steps taken by its designers is to determine what instructions the computer will execute. The most important factor influencing the selection of instructions is the intended use of the machine. If the computer was intended to manage a telephone switching system, for example, its instruction repertoire would be far different than that of a computer intended for scientific applications.

Up to now we have used only a few very simple computer instructions to illustrate how some units of the computer work. Most computers have a wide range of instructions in their repertoire, however, and this unit will describe them and show how they are used.

Computer instructions are generally grouped into classes according to their function. For example, all those that perform binary arithmetic are in the arithmetic class, those that cause an instruction to be executed out of sequence are called the branch- or jump-class instructions, and those that cause information to be stored in memory are called store-class instructions.

Each instruction is given a short name to indicate its function—Branch on Zero, for example—but even this name is too long for programming use. The name is shortened to a three- or four-letter mnemonic (meaning *"intended to assist memory"*) such as BRZ for Branch on Zero, and a programmer writes BRZ when this instruction is to be used.

A TYPICAL INSTRUCTION REPERTOIRE

Given in the following pages is a description of an instruction set that is typical of that used by a small-to-medium general-purpose computer. Some of the instructions have been simplified in order to illustrate principles of operation rather than the electronic details, but all the essential information has been retained.

"Repertoire" is a clumsy word to use in everyday conversation, so most people dealing with computers call the group of instructions that a computer can execute its "instruction set." The instructions are divided

into classes by function, and that is the way in which we will present the instruction descriptions. In general, the descriptions proceed from the simplest instructions to the most complex.

The following is a list of instructions in the set of our typical computer. A three-letter mnemonic representing the instruction is given first; this is followed by the full name of the instruction. A letter (N) also appears in some instructions in the list. Commonly used to indicate that a number to be chosen by the user will appear in this position, it means, in our case, that the number of an index register to be used with this instruction will replace the "N" in actual use.

Special Class
HLT	Halt

Load Class
LDA	Load Accumulator
LAR	Load A Register
LDX (N)	Load Index Register (N)

Store Class
STO	Store Accumulator
STA	Store A Register
STQ	Store MQ Register
STZ	Store Zero
STX (N)	Store Index Register (N)

Arithmetic Class
CAD	Clear and Add
ADD	Add
SUB	Subtract
MUL	Multiply
DIV	Divide
ADX (N)	Add Index Register (N)
CPA	Compare Accumulator
CPX (N)	Compare Index Register (N)

Logical Class
AND	Logical AND
IOR	Inclusive OR
XOR	Exclusive OR

Modify Index Register Class
DIX (N)	Decrement Index Register (N)
IIX (N)	Increment Index Register (N)
TIX (N)	Test Index Register (N)

Shift Class
SHR	Shift Right, Open
SRC	Shift Right, Closed
SHL	Shift Left, Open
SLC	Shift Left, Closed
DSR	Double Shift Right, Open
DSC	Double Shift Right, Closed
DSL	Double Shift Left, Open
DLC	Double Shift Left, Closed

Branch and Jump Class
BRE	Branch on Equal
BRP	Branch on Positive
BRN	Branch on Negative
BRZ	Branch on Zero
BRU	Branch Unconditional
BPI (N)	Branch on Positive Index (N)
BNI (N)	Branch on Negative Index (N)
TLJ	Test Literal and Jump
TMJ	Test Mask and Jump
JUC	Jump Unconditional

Stack and Exit Class
SBU	Stack and Branch Unconditional
SBP	Stack and Branch on Positive
SBN	Stack and Branch on Negative
SPX (N)	Stack and Branch on Positive Index (N)
SNX (N)	Stack and Branch on Negative Index (N)
EXU	Exit Unconditional
EXB	Exit and Branch
EXP	Exit on Positive
EXN	Exit on Negative

Input/Output Class
RSS	Read Sense Switches
RKB	Read Keyboard
TMV	Tape Movement
RMT	Read Magnetic Tape
WMT	Write Magnetic Tape
ADK	Address Disk
RDK	Read Disk
WDK	Write Disk
PRT	Print
RCR	Read from Card Reader
WDP	Write to Display
SEC	Select Communications
RDC	Read Communications
WRC	Write Communications

INSTRUCTION FORMATS

For the purpose of this discussion, it is assumed that the computer with the instruction set listed earlier is a single-address machine. Single address means that only one memory address is included in the instruction. Therefore, the instruction format for this computer would be that shown in Figure 31.

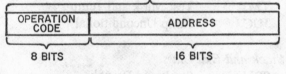

Figure 31. Typical Instruction Format

The reason for the division of eight bits for operation code and sixteen bits for address is a simple one: Only eight bits are required to hold all possible operation codes in the instruction set, but the computer has the capability of providing 65,536 memory locations, requiring a sixteen-bit address to select one.

Called the operation code because it is a number telling the computer what operation it is to perform, the eight-bit code in our example would be read as an octal or hexadecimal number. We have chosen the octal system for ease of reading.

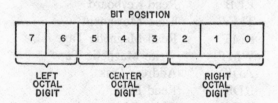

Figure 32. Division of the Operation Code

The eight-bit code is divided into three octal digits as shown in Figure 32. Note that the left octal digit has only two related bit positions, so it can be only 0, 1, 2, or 3.

When operation codes are assigned to each of the instructions, we arrive at the following list:

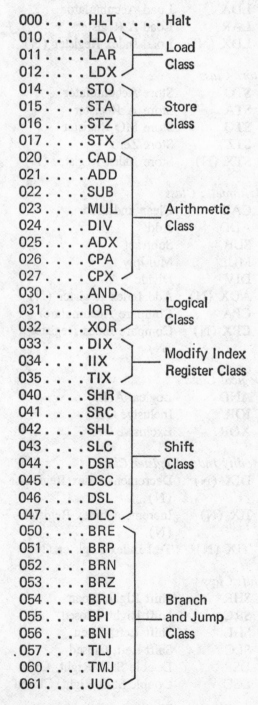

000 . . . . HLT . . . . Halt		
010 . . . . LDA	⎫	
011 . . . . LAR	⎬ Load Class	
012 . . . . LDX	⎭	
014 . . . . STO	⎫	
015 . . . . STA	⎬ Store Class	
016 . . . . STZ		
017 . . . . STX	⎭	
020 . . . . CAD	⎫	
021 . . . . ADD		
022 . . . . SUB		
023 . . . . MUL	⎬ Arithmetic Class	
024 . . . . DIV		
025 . . . . ADX		
026 . . . . CPA		
027 . . . . CPX	⎭	
030 . . . . AND	⎫	
031 . . . . IOR	⎬ Logical Class	
032 . . . . XOR	⎭	
033 . . . . DIX	⎫	
034 IIX	⎬ Modify Index Register Class	
035 . . . . TIX	⎭	
040 . . . . SHR	⎫	
041 . . . . SRC		
042 . . . . SHL		
043 . . . . SLC	⎬ Shift Class	
044 . . . . DSR		
045 . . . . DSC		
046 . . . . DSL		
047 . . . . DLC	⎭	
050 . . . . BRE	⎫	
051 . . . . BRP		
052 . . . . BRN		
053 . . . . BRZ		
054 . . . . BRU	⎬ Branch and Jump Class	
055 . . . . BPI		
056 . . . . BNI		
057 . . . . TLJ		
060 . . . . TMJ		
061 . . . . JUC	⎭	

070 . . . . SBU		
071 . . . . SBP		
072 . . . . SBN		
073 . . . . SPX	Stack	
074 . . . . SNX	and Exit	
075 . . . . EXU	Class	
076 . . . . EXB		
077 . . . . EXP		
100 . . . . EXN		
110 . . . . RSS		
111 . . . . RKB		
11N . . . . TMV		
12N . . . . RMT		
12N . . . . WMT		
127 . . . . ADK		
130 . . . . RDK	I/O Class	
134 . . . . WDK		
14N . . . . PRT		
15N . . . . RCR		
16N . . . . WDP		
20N . . . . SEC		
210 . . . . RDC		
220 . . . . WRC		

Examination of the operation codes reveals some patterns. Instructions within a class usually bear related numbers. For example, shifts are all in the 04N group. In addition, the very complex I/O operations, 110 through 220 in our instruction set, usually have many combinations available in the right octal digit; this is done so that the details of the instruction can be added by the programmer and control unit. This possibility will be discussed when the input/output instruction class is described later in this unit.

While the three-letter mnemonic does help a computer programmer or service technician remember the instruction set, there are obviously too many names and codes for all to be memorized. Most computer manufacturers provide a small "code card," often covered with plastic, to assist the user. It includes the mnemonic, the full instruction name, the octal code, and other information useful in programming and locating machine failures.

THE HALT INSTRUCTION

Once started, a computer continues to execute instructions until stopped by a halt instruction or by some external signal such as a switch on a control panel. A halt instruction is given at the end of a program and at certain points in a program where operator intervention is required. When a program is being tested for the first time, for example, the programmer may place halt instructions at critical points in the program so that he can examine the results of executing one section of the program at a time.

The format of the halt instruction in our typical instruction set is shown in Figure 33. Note that the halt instruction has an operation code of all 0s, and the address is of no significance; hence Xs are placed in the address position. ("X" is generally used to mean "don't care.") A halt instruction brings the computer to a stop, with the instruction address of the next instruction to be executed in the instruction address counter. Manual action to restart is required, and a push button is usually provided.

Use of an operation code of all zeros for the halt instruction is common. A failure that prevented an instruction from reaching the control unit could result in an operation code of all 0s in the instruction register. If this code is assigned to halt rather than to another instruction, the machine will stop when such a failure occurs.

000	XXXXXX

HLT – HALT

Figure 33. Format of the Halt Instruction

LOAD- AND STORE-CLASS INSTRUCTIONS

These two classes of instructions are discussed together because they have the common function of moving data between the arithmetic unit and memory. Load-class instructions extract the contents of a

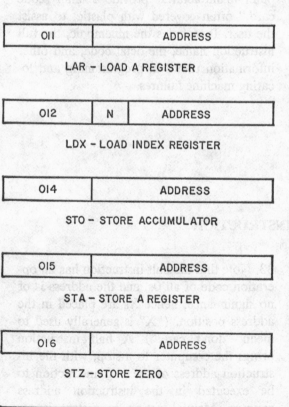

Figure 34. Formats of Load- and Store-class Instructions

specific memory location and move them to a register in the arithmetic unit. Conversely, store-class instructions move the contents of a certain register into a specific memory location.

In our typical instruction set, we have three load-class instructions and four store-class instructions. The formats appear in Figure 34, and descriptions of each follow.

LDA—Load Accumulator

The contents of the memory location selected by the address are loaded into the accumulator directly, without passing through the A register.

LAR—Load A Register

The contents of the memory location selected by the address are loaded into the A register.

LDX(N)—Load Index Register (N)

The contents of the memory location selected by the address are loaded into index register N. Note that three bits of the address portion of the instruction specify the index register, so only thirteen bits are left for the memory address in this instruction. Some computers use a variation of this instruction in which the number to be loaded into the index register replaces the address portion of the instruction, and thus memory access is not required.

STO—Store Accumulator

The contents of the accumulator are stored in the memory location selected by the address.

STA—Store A Register

The contents of the A register are stored in the memory location selected by the address.

STQ—Store MQ Register

The contents of the MQ register are stored in the memory location selected by the address.

STZ—Store Zero

All 0s are stored in the memory location selected by the address. (This is one way of assuring that a memory location is cleared if it is desired to accumulate a count whose value is unknown.)

STX(N)—Store Index Register (N)

The contents of the index register selected by N are stored in the memory location chosen by the address. Note that three bits are used to choose N, leaving only thirteen bits for the address.

ARITHMETIC-CLASS INSTRUCTIONS

Included in this class are the instructions that perform the binary arithmetic discussed in Unit 1. These instructions are the ones that do the actual "computing." Most of the others in the instruction set serve to obtain data for the arithmetic unit and to store the results.

There are eight instructions in the arithmetic class of our typical set. The formats are shown in Figure 35, and descriptions follow.

CAD—Clear and Add

The accumulator is cleared and the contents of the memory location selected by the address are added, effectively replacing the current accumulator contents. This instruction differs from the LDA—Load Accumulator—in that the information passes through the A register in this instruction, destroying its contents, while the LDA instruction moves the information directly to the accumulator.

ADD—Add

The contents of the memory location selected by the address are added to the current contents of the accumulator, and the sum appears in the accumulator. The information to be added passes through the A register.

SUB—Subtract

The contents of the memory location selected by the address are subtracted from the accumulator and the difference appears in the accumulator. The information to be subtracted passes through the A register.

MUL—Multiply

The contents of the accumulator are multiplied by the contents of the memory location selected by the address. At completion, the more significant half of the double-length product appears in the accumulator, and the MQ register holds the less significant half. The multiplier remains in the A register.

DIV—Divide

A double-length dividend held in the accumulator and MQ register is divided by the contents of the memory location selected by the address. The divisor is held in the A register. The quotient appears in the MQ register, and the remainder appears in the accumulator.

ADX(N)—Add Index Register (N)

The contents of the index register selected by "N" are added to the contents of the accumulator, and the sum appears in the accumulator.

CPA—Compare Accumulator

The contents of the memory location selected by the address are compared to the current contents of the accumulator. The "high" indicator is set if the accumulator is greater, the "equal" indicator is set if they are equal, and the "low" indicator is set if the accumulator contents are less. Values being compared are left unchanged.

CPX(N)—Compare Index Register (N)

The contents of the index register chosen by "N" are compared with the contents of the memory location selected by the address. The "high" indicator is set if the index register is greater, the "equal" indicator is set if they are equal, and the "low" indicator is set if the index register is less. Values being compared are left unchanged.

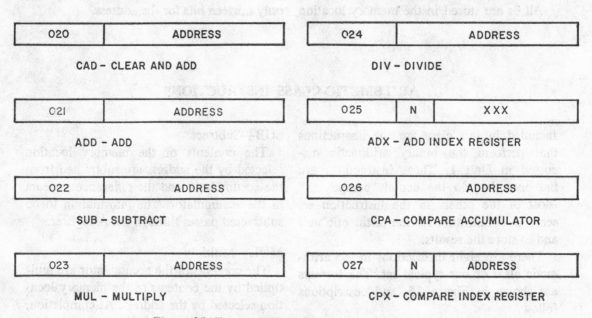

Figure 35. Formats of Arithmetic-class Instructions

LOGICAL-CLASS INSTRUCTIONS

Three "logical" operations (Logical AND, Inclusive OR, and Exclusive OR) were discussed in the description of binary arithmetic given in Unit 1. Instructions in the logical class of our typical set perform those operations.

While most readers should be able to understand the intended use of the instructions described up to now, the application of the logical-class instructions is not immediately apparent to those without some computer experience. So first we will illustrate one typical use of these instructions.

The logical-class instructions are frequently used to test an unknown quantity. It has been assumed up to now that our typical computer handles bytes as its basic units of information; therefore we will use the contents of a byte as the unknown quantity to be tested.

As an example, we will test a single bit of a byte to see if it is a 1 or a 0. Often a byte called a status byte is provided to the computer by a peripheral unit to describe the conditions existing in the peripheral unit. One bit of such a status byte from a magnetic tape unit could indicate that the tape is at the load point—that is, fully rewound. The computer needs to know this before beginning tape operations, so it needs to test the "at-load point" bit of the status byte.

We begin testing after the status byte has been placed in the accumulator by other instructions and, for purposes of this discussion, we designate bit position 7 as the "at-load point" bit. Established in memory is a "mask" byte with a 1 in bit position 7 and 0s in positions 0 through 6. Call this the "load-point mask." A Logical AND instruction is then executed to perform a logical AND operation between the status byte in the accumulator and the load-point mask.

Each bit in the mask is matched against the corresponding bit in the status byte. Only when both bits in a given position being matched are 1s is a 1 placed in the same position of the accumulator. Since bits 0 through 6 of the mask are 0s, positions 0 through 6 of the accumulator are made 0s regardless of the status byte contents.

Bit 7 of the mask is a 1, however, so bit position 7 (the "at-load point" bit) of the status byte will determine the final setting of bit 7 of the accumulator. If the tape is at the load point, position 7 of the accumulator will be a 1 when the instruction is finished; if not, position 7 will be a 0. Thus, if the accumulator is all 0s, the tape is not at load point and a rewind command must be issued. On the other hand, if the accumulator is not all 0s, the computer can proceed with tape operations without rewinding. How the accumulator is tested for 0s will be explained in the description of branch-class instructions later in this section.

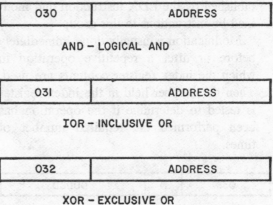

AND – LOGICAL AND

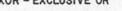

IOR – INCLUSIVE OR

XOR – EXCLUSIVE OR

Figure 36. Formats of Logical-class Instructions

Formats of the logical-class instructions are shown in Figure 36, and descriptions of these instructions appear below.

AND—Logical AND

The contents of the memory location chosen by the address are logically ANDed with the current contents of the accumulator, and the results are placed in the accumulator.

IOR—Inclusive OR

The contents of the memory location chosen by the address are logically ORed with the current contents of the accumulator, and the results are placed in the accumulator.

XOR—Exclusive OR

The contents of the memory location chosen by the address are combined with the current contents of the accumulator in an Exclusive OR operation, and the results are placed in the accumulator.

MODIFY INDEX REGISTER-CLASS INSTRUCTIONS

Two of the three instructions in this class are intended to give the programmer control of the index register contents. Recall that there was a LDX—Load Index Register—instruction among those in the load class; so the index register contents are established by the LDX instruction and modified by instructions in this group.

Modification is usually done immediately before or after a repetitive operation in which the index register contents are used. Then the number held in the index register is tested to determine if the operation has been performed the required number of times.

033	N	DDDDD

DIX – DECREMENT INDEX REGISTER

034	N	IIIII

IIX – INCREMENT INDEX REGISTER

035	N	PPPPP

TIX – TEST INDEX REGISTER

Figure 37. Formats of Modify Index Register-class Instructions

Shown in Figure 37 are the formats of the instructions in this class. Note that three positions are occupied by the index register number, so only thirteen positions are available for the rest of the operand.

DIX(N)—Decrement Index Register (N)

The number in the "D" positions is subtracted from index register N, and the difference is returned to the index register.

IIX(N)—Increment Index Register (N)

The number in the "I" positions is added to index register N, and the sum is returned to the index register.

TIX(N)—Test Index Register (N)

The contents of the index register selected by N are compared against the number in the "P" positions. If they are not equal, the next instruction is executed in the normal, sequential order. If they are equal, the next instruction is skipped.

SHIFT-CLASS INSTRUCTIONS

The purpose of the instructions in this group is to move a number laterally so that each bit of the number moves into another bit position. Uses of these instructions are many and varied. A number may be shifted, for example, until all bits of that number but one have been moved out of a register. Then that register can be tested for 0, and the results of that test will indicate whether the remaining bit is a 1 or a 0. Regardless of the specific use, the instructions in the shift class all have one common purpose: to move information in the arithmetic unit's primary registers so that it can be operated on more effectively.

Figure 38 illustrates the paths over which data can be shifted by the instructions in the shift class. It shows that the accumulator and MQ registers can be linked and that each register can be a closed loop, with bits leaving one end and re-entering the other end.

All shift-class instructions use the same format, that being the operation code in the left eight bits and the shift count in the right sixteen bits, as shown in Figure 39. Obviously eight shifts are the maximum required before a number is moved completely out of our eight-bit registers, so most of the shift-count positions are unused.

The following paragraphs describe the action taken by each shift instruction. Relate the paths followed to the diagram in Figure 38 when reading each description.

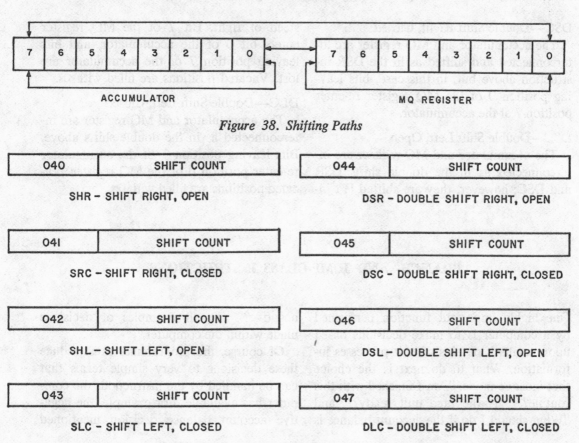

Figure 38. Shifting Paths

Figure 39. Formats of Shift-class Instructions

SHR—Shift Right, Open

The accumulator is shifted right (bit 7 toward bit 0) by the number in the shift count. Bits leaving position 0 are lost. Vacated positions are filled with 0s.

SRC—Shift Right, Closed

The accumulator is shifted right (bit 7 toward bit 0) by the number in the shift count. Bits leaving position 0 re-enter position 7. Closed shifts are also called "circular" in some machines.

SHL—Shift Left, Open

The accumulator is shifted left (bit 0 toward bit 7) by the number in the shift count. Bits leaving position 7 are lost. Vacated positions are filled with 0s.

SLC—Shift Left, Closed

The accumulator is shifted left (bit 0 toward bit 7) by the number in the shift count. Bits leaving position 7 re-enter position 0.

DSR—Double Shift Right, Open

The accumulator and MQ register are connected to form a double-length register. (Bit 0 of the accumulator is connected to bit 7 of the MQ register.) Both registers are shifted right by the number in the shift count. Bits leaving position 0 of the accumulator enter position 7 of the MQ register. Bits leaving position 0 of the MQ register are lost. Vacated positions are filled with 0s.

DSC—Double Shift Right, Closed

The accumulator and MQ register are interconnected and shifted as in the DSR instruction above but, in this case, bits leaving position 0 of the MQ register re-enter position 7 of the accumulator.

DSL—Double Shift Left, Open

The accumulator and MQ register are interconnected as in the double shifts DSR and DSC; however, they are shifted left instead of right. Bit 7 of the MQ register enters bit 0 of the accumulator, and bits leaving position 7 of the accumulator are lost. Vacated positions are filled with 0s.

DLC—Double Shift Left, Closed

The accumulator and MQ register are interconnected as in the double shifts above. Bits leaving position 7 of the accumulator re-enter position 0 of the MQ register. Vacated positions are filled with 0s.

BRANCH- AND JUMP-CLASS INSTRUCTIONS

One highly important function performed by a computer is to make decisions based upon results it obtains after it processes information. What to do next is the choice that must be made. "Am I finished with this routine?," "Is the tape unit ready?," and "What should I do if the account balance is negative?" are all examples of decisions made within the computer.

Of course, the programmer must reduce these decisions to very simple terms that can be handled by the instructions the computer has available. For example, the negative account balance decision mentioned

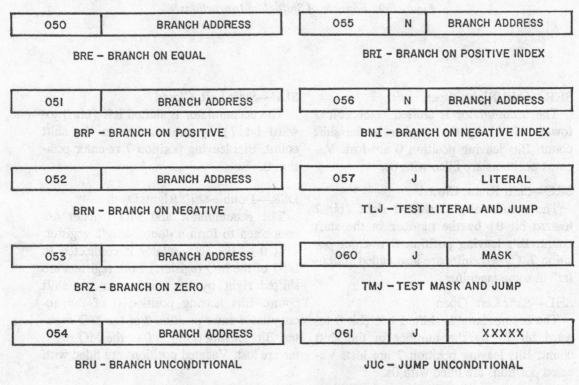

Figure 40. Formats of Branch- and Jump-class Instructions

above would probably be made after examination of the sign of the number held in the accumulator.

Instructions available to make tests and decisions are those in the branch and jump class covered in this section and the stack and exit instructions covered in the next section. Most make a simple test of the contents of the accumulator or index register after the programmer has prepared for the test.

There are ten instructions in the branch and jump class of our typical instruction set. Each differs from the others somewhat in execution but all produce the same effect: They cause the contents of the instruction-address counter to be replaced by a new address, thus "branching" or "jumping" to another part of the computer program. At the new address is the first instruction of the routine necessary to take the action required by the decision just made.

Formats of the instructions in this class are shown in Figure 40, and each instruction is described below.

BRE—Branch on Equal

This instruction tests the "equal" indicator set by the CPA and CPX instructions. If the "equal" indicator is on, the branch address replaces the current contents of the instruction-address counter. If the equal indicator is off, the instruction-address counter is left unchanged.

BRP—Branch on Positive

This instruction could operate in either of two ways, depending upon whether "signed" registers are used and whether or not the CPA and CPX instructions are in the instruction set. Assume first that "signed" registers are used. In this case, the BRP instruction examines the sign of the accumulator. Finding it positive (a 0), it causes the branch by replacing the contents of the instruction-address counter with the branch address.

Assume next that unsigned registers are used but the CPA instruction is included in the set. In this case, the BRP instruction tests the state of the "high" indicator, which was set if the accumulator was found to be greater in the comparison operation. If the "high" indicator was set, the branch takes place.

BRN—Branch on Negative

This instruction operates in the same manner as the BRP except that it tests for a negative sign (a 1) of the accumulator or the "low" indicator being set by the CPA instruction.

BRZ—Branch on Zero

This instruction tests the contents of the accumulator. If the accumulator is all 0s, the branch is made.

BRU—Branch Unconditional

This instruction places the branch address in the instruction-address counter, automatically causing the branch to take place.

BPI(N)—Branch on Positive Index (N)

This instruction tests the sign of the index register chosen by N. If it is positive (a 0), the branch takes place.

BNI(N)—Branch on Negative Index (N)

This instruction tests the sign of the index register chosen by N. If it is negative (a 1), the branch takes place.

TLJ—Test Literal and Jump

This instruction compares the contents of the accumulator with a number called the "literal." If they are equal, the value in J (four positions and a sign) is added to or subtracted from the contents of the instruction-address counter. This enables a jump forward or backward of up to fifteen instructions.

TMJ—Test Mask and Jump

This instruction tests each bit of the accumulator designated by the mask. If the mask bit in a given position (bit 2, for example) is a 1, the corresponding position of the accumulator is tested for a 1. When all tested positions are 1s, the jump is made by adding or subtracting the jump value in "J" to the instruction-address counter. If any of the bits tested is a 0, the jump is not made.

JUC—Jump Unconditional

The value in "J" is automatically added to or subtracted from the instruction-address counter to cause the jump to take place.

STACK- AND EXIT-CLASS INSTRUCTIONS

A single branch and its accompanying return are usually no problems for a programmer, but when several branches may take place in succession before the program returns to the point at which the first branch occurred, it becomes very difficult for the programmer to handle instruction addresses. Therefore, most modern computers provide registers in which addresses "branched from" can be automatically stored and retrieved. This group of registers is called the "instruction address stack," which is abbreviated IAS for the rest of this description.

Assume that the IAS consists of sixteen registers. This would allow sixteen "branched from" addresses to be held. The newest branched-from address is the last in and first out of the stack, and the oldest branched-from address is the first in and last out. This section describes the instructions used to control the stack; instruction formats are shown in Figure 41.

SBU—Stack and Branch Unconditional

This instruction stores the current contents of the instruction-address counter in the top position of the IAS, forcing down all other stored "branched from" addresses. It then places the branch address in the instruction-address counter, causing the branch to take place.

SBP—Stack and Branch on Positive

This instruction tests the same conditions as the BRP—Branch on Positive—instruction described earlier. If it finds that the tested condition is met, it stores the contents of the instruction-address counter in the IAS and places the branch address in the counter, causing the branch to take place.

SBN—Stack and Branch on Negative

This instruction tests the same conditions as BRN—Branch on Negative, which was also described earlier. If it finds that the tested condition is met, it stores the contents of the instruction-address counter in the IAS and places the branch address in the counter, causing the branch to take place.

SPX(N)—Stack and Branch on Positive Index (N)

This instruction tests the sign of the index register specified by N. If the sign is positive, the stack and branch operation takes place.

SNX(N)—Stack and Branch on Negative Index (N)

This instruction tests the sign of the index register specified by N. If the sign is negative, the stack and branch operation takes place.

EXU—Exit Unconditional

An exit instruction is the way in which the computer returns from a stack and branch operation. Assume that the computer executed a stack and branch operation that led to a short program to sort numbers and place them in numerical order. When the sorting was completed, the objective is to return to the point at which the branch took place. This is done very simply by an Exit Unconditional instruction.

The EXU instruction causes the latest "branched from" address, now held in the top register of the IAS, to be returned to the instruction-address counter. Of course, this causes the program to return to the point at which the branch took place. The counter is stepped up by one after it is loaded so that the program actually resumes at one instruction after the original branch instruction. When the branched-from address is moved from the stack, all other addresses in the stack are moved up by one.

EXP—Exit on Positive, and EXN—Exit on Negative

These two instructions perform the same exit function as EXU—Exit Unconditional, except that they first test the sign of the accumulator for positive (EXP) or negative (EXN) and make the exit only if they find the condition for which they are testing.

EXB—Exit and Branch

This instruction performs a combination of an unconditional exit and a branch. First, the IAS stack is moved up, causing the latest "branched from" address to "pop off" the top. In other exit instructions, this address is moved into the instruction-address counter but, in EXB, it is not. Instead, the branch address from this instruction is placed in the instruction-address counter.

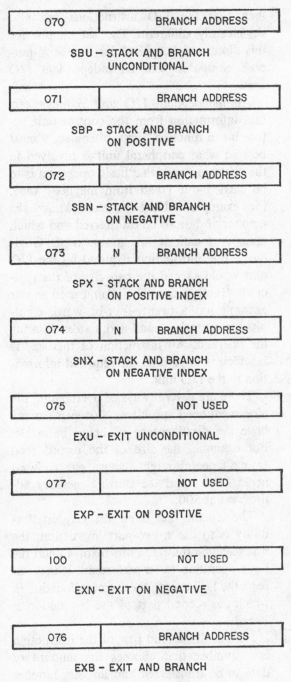

Figure 41. Formats of Stack and Exit Instructions

INPUT/OUTPUT-CLASS INSTRUCTIONS

When we were discussing input/output units earlier, it was pointed out that input/output units differ greatly from one computer to the next. It logically follows then that the I/O instructions are also significantly different. The set chosen for this discussion is typical for a general-purpose computer with an independent I/O unit.

An independent I/O unit requires certain information from the control unit before it can function. First, of course, it must be told what peripheral unit is involved in the operation and what basic operation is to be carried out (read from magnetic tape, for example). Next it must know the amount of data to be transferred and which memory locations are to be used. Obviously, the information required by the I/O unit would exceed the capacity of the typical instruction size. The format used as our example has a twenty-four-bit-word, eight-bits-for-operation code and sixteen bits for the operand. An instruction of this size is insufficient to give all the required information to the I/O unit.

There are several ways of overcoming the aforementioned problem; however, many have the disadvantage of being inflexible. For example, the size of the record read from a tape unit might always be established at 256 bytes and the starting memory address set at 500.

The scheme that offers the greatest flexibility is to use a two-part instruction, the first selecting the I/O units involved and the basic operation to be performed. It then directs the I/O unit to the memory location in which the second part of the instruction is stored.

Held in the second part of the instruction is a number that chooses the amount of data to be transferred and another number that chooses the memory location in which data transfer is to begin. This scheme is called the input/output control command (IOCC). A typical instruction using the IOCC scheme is the RMT—Read Magnetic Tape—instruction, which is shown at the top of Figure 42.

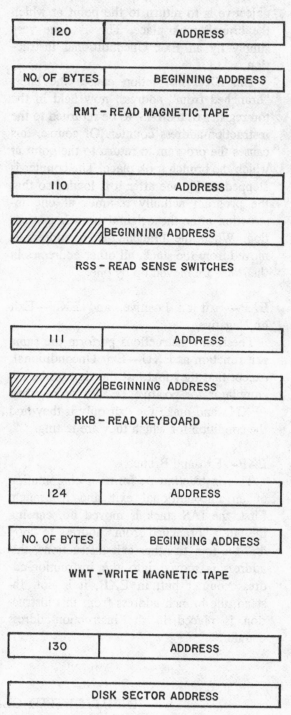

Figure 42.
Formats of Input-Output-class Instructions

RMT – READ MAGNETIC TAPE

RSS – READ SENSE SWITCHES

RKB – READ KEYBOARD

WMT – WRITE MAGNETIC TAPE

ADK – ADDRESS DISK

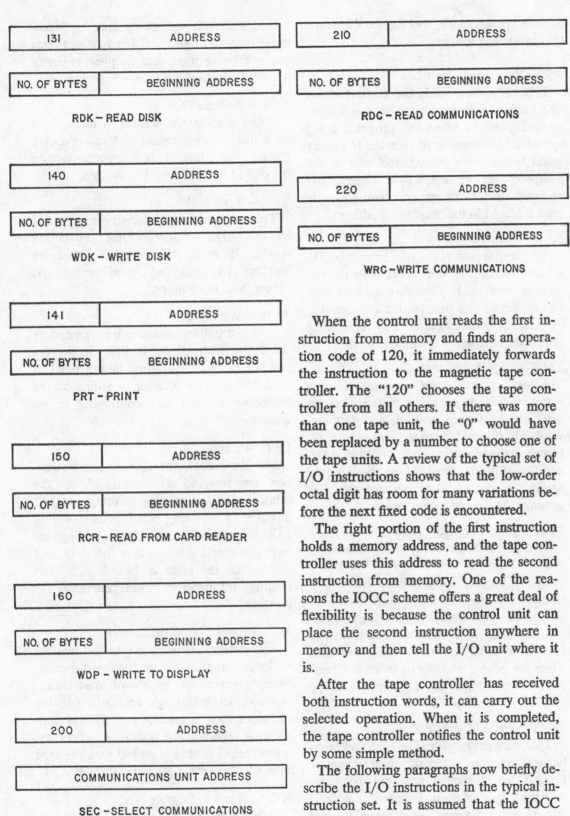

131	ADDRESS

NO. OF BYTES	BEGINNING ADDRESS

RDK – READ DISK

140	ADDRESS

NO. OF BYTES	BEGINNING ADDRESS

WDK – WRITE DISK

141	ADDRESS

NO. OF BYTES	BEGINNING ADDRESS

PRT – PRINT

150	ADDRESS

NO. OF BYTES	BEGINNING ADDRESS

RCR – READ FROM CARD READER

160	ADDRESS

NO. OF BYTES	BEGINNING ADDRESS

WDP – WRITE TO DISPLAY

200	ADDRESS

COMMUNICATIONS UNIT ADDRESS

SEC – SELECT COMMUNICATIONS

210	ADDRESS

NO. OF BYTES	BEGINNING ADDRESS

RDC – READ COMMUNICATIONS

220	ADDRESS

NO. OF BYTES	BEGINNING ADDRESS

WRC – WRITE COMMUNICATIONS

When the control unit reads the first instruction from memory and finds an operation code of 120, it immediately forwards the instruction to the magnetic tape controller. The "120" chooses the tape controller from all others. If there was more than one tape unit, the "0" would have been replaced by a number to choose one of the tape units. A review of the typical set of I/O instructions shows that the low-order octal digit has room for many variations before the next fixed code is encountered.

The right portion of the first instruction holds a memory address, and the tape controller uses this address to read the second instruction from memory. One of the reasons the IOCC scheme offers a great deal of flexibility is because the control unit can place the second instruction anywhere in memory and then tell the I/O unit where it is.

After the tape controller has received both instruction words, it can carry out the selected operation. When it is completed, the tape controller notifies the control unit by some simple method.

The following paragraphs now briefly describe the I/O instructions in the typical instruction set. It is assumed that the IOCC scheme applies to all, and Figure 42 shows the instruction formats.

RSS—Read Sense Switches

This instruction reads the current status of a bank of switches placed on a computer control panel to affect the program being operated. The number of switches is usually equal to the basic information unit in the computer—in our case, a byte. The number of bytes read is always one, and the byte read is placed in the "beginning address."

RKB—Read Keyboard

This instruction reads one keystroke (in a code, of course) and places it in the beginning address. Keyboards are often read one keystroke at a time so that the meaning of each key can be examined by the control unit before the next keystroke is read.

TMV—Tape Movement

This instruction selects a tape unit and provides commands to be executed. Among these are backspace, rewind, and fast forward. The format is not shown in Figure 42, however, the operation code would be 11N, and the digit in the "N" position would specify the command to be executed. For example, 113 could mean "rewind."

RMT—Read Magnetic Tape

This instruction reads a specified number of bytes from one tape unit. The first byte is placed in the beginning address and subsequent bytes in successive addresses. Although the tape always moves one full record, the number of bytes does not have to be a full record. The control unit is notified when the proper number of bytes has been read, even though the tape may still be moving.

WMT—Write Magnetic Tape

This instruction writes the specified number of bytes in a record on a magnetic tape. Once a record size has been established, it is often maintained at a fixed size. If this is the case, the number of bytes specified must be equal to the established record size, although many may be "dummies" (unused bytes). If fixed record sizes are not being used, the number of bytes specified constitutes a complete record.

ADK—Address Disk

When reading and writing is to be done on a disk, the individual sectors on a disk are addressed first. This instruction locates the disk sector to be read or written.

RDK—Read Disk

This instruction must have been preceded by the ADK—Address Disk instruction above. It reads the number of bytes specified from the addressed sector and places them in memory.

WDK—Write Disk

This instruction must also be preceded by the ADK instruction. It then writes the number of bytes specified, taking the first from the memory location specified by the beginning address and continuing in sequence.

PRT—Print

The low-order octal digits in this instruction are reserved for commands to the printer, with 141 causing printing and 142 through 147 causing other printer action; 142, for example, could be a carriage-return command. Only when the I/O unit senses that the code is 141 does it start reading information from memory for printing.

RCR—Read from Card Reader

This instruction reads a specified number of bytes from cards in the card reader. Note, however, that each card must always pass completely through the reader whether all information is read or not. This is similar to a tape-reading operation where the entire record is always moved past the read head whether or not all bytes in it are read.

WDP—Write to Display

This instruction is used to load the memory of a display unit and update portions of the display as required. The low-order octal digit also can carry other commands. Perhaps 165 would be "clear screen." Only when the code was 160 would the I/O unit carry out the data transfer necessary to provide a display.

SEC—Select Communications

This instruction performs a function similar to the ADK—Address Disk instruction; it chooses the address of the communications device involved. Note also that the low-order octal digit can be used to give

commands. Assume, for example, that 204 could be a clear command.

RDC—Read Communications

This instruction reads a specified number of bytes from a communications channel, such as voice-grade telephone lines, and places them in memory.

WRC—Write Communications

This instruction sends the specified number of bytes over a communications channel, the first byte being taken from the beginning address.

QUIZ ON THE SUBJECT MATTER IN UNIT 3

1. What is the relationship between a computer's intended use and its instruction set?

2. Why is a mnemonic used to represent an instruction?

3. What are the two parts of an instruction format?

4. What determines the size of the operation code field?

5. What generally determines the size of the operand field?

6. What is the meaning of the letter "N" when it is used in the operation code or operand field?

7. What is the relationship between the operation codes of all the instructions in a specific class?

8. What is the meaning of the letter "X" when it is used in either the operation code or operand fields?

9. Describe the conditions that exist in the computer after the halt instruction is executed.

10. What is the function of load-class instructions?
Of store-class instructions?

11. Arithmetic-class instructions include those that perform all four basic mathematical operations ($+$, $-$, $\times$, $\div$). If an instruction set did not include multiply and divide, how could the computer be made to perform multiplication and division?

12. What is one of the primary uses of the logical-class instructions?

13. When are index register contents usually modified and tested?

14. Describe a circular, or closed, shift and how it differs from an "open" shift.

15. All branch- and jump-class instructions have one common function. What is it?

16. What is the advantage of having "stack" and "exit" instructions in a computer's instruction set?

17. Why is the IOCC (Input/output control command) scheme used in many computers?

UNIT 4

THE PROGRAMS

As more computers are sold for home use, many of us will become computer programmers. Of course, the ultimate in ease of programming would be a machine that could accept voice commands from the user and respond with complex actions. Even in this case, however, the user would have to state his requirements in some logical sequence in order to get the job done properly, and that is the essence of programming—giving commands to which the computer can respond and giving them in the proper order.

This unit takes the reader from a definition of what programming is through the construction of a sample program. It discusses the use of "high level" languages to give instructions. These "near English"

languages are now in use and are undoubtedly the form in which home computer users will program their machines. Unit 4 also discusses how a programmer begins to organize his program, showing the set of symbols that are commonly used to describe program actions and sequences.

The quiz at the end of Unit 4 differs somewhat from those in earlier units. Though it begins with "recall" questions—those in which the reader is expected to answer the question from memory—the Unit 4 quiz includes several sample programming problems, each of which may be solved in a variety of ways. One solution to each problem is given to illustrate the way in which programming is done.

INTRODUCTION TO PROGRAMMING

The word "programming" means to select and place in the proper order the instructions required to cause a computer to perform a specific task. Only the instructions in the instruction repertoire are available, but they may be used in any order and in any number necessary for the task.

As a first step to learning more about programming it is necessary to become familiar with terms used. Let's begin with "machine code" or "machine language."

It was pointed out earlier that a computer is capable of handling only 1s and 0s internally; therefore all information, including instructions that make up a program, must be reduced to binary form. An instruction in its binary form is the machine code or language.

Examine one of the instructions in the typical instruction set as it would appear in machine code. The instruction is Load Accumulator, which would appear as follows:

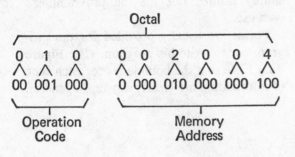

Octal

Operation Code / Memory Address

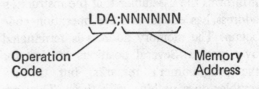

LDA;NNNNNN

Operation Code / Memory Address

The memory address shown could be any number, but the operation code must always be as shown.

Obviously, writing all these 1s and 0s would be a burden on the programmer, so a simpler way was devised soon after computers were developed. That way involved the use of very complex programs called assemblers and compilers to read a higher-level language written by the programmer and convert that language into machine code. The finished product produced by the assembler or compiler program is a machine-code program that can be accepted and executed by a computer.

The distinction between assembler and compiler programs has become less pronounced in recent years. Originally, an assembler produced one machine-code instruction for each instruction provided by the programmer, while a compiler may have produced several machine-code instructions as required to carry out a single instruction given by the programmer. This is still true in many cases. In general, however, the process of converting the programmer's instructions into machine code is called assembly, and the programs that perform this function are called assemblers.

The language in which a programmer provides his inputs to an assembly program is generally one step removed from the machine code and, logically, it is called assembler language. Examine the Load Accumulator instruction written in assembler language.

The operation code is given in mnemonic form; it is converted to 00001000 by the assembler program. Next comes punctuation to separate types of information. In this case, the assembler program recognizes a semicolon (;) as the end of the operation code and the beginning of the address.

Addresses written in assembler language are almost always written in symbolic form —that is, absolute numbers are not used. In the example above, the memory location has been designated NNNNNN. Another location might be NNNNNN+1. Only the relative location need be provided as an input to the assembler; the assembler assigns the absolute numbers to the locations.

The instruction written in assembler language is usually called a "source statement," and it may include other information. For example:

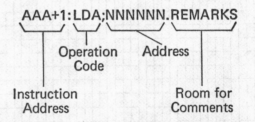

AAA+1:LDA;NNNNNN.REMARKS

Instruction Address / Operation Code / Address / Room for Comments

Shown above is an address in which the programmer wants the LDA instruction to be placed. Notice that it is given in a symbolic form rather than as an absolute location number. Location AAA will be assigned a number by the assembler program (for example, 0200); then the LDA instruction will be placed in the following location (201 in this case).

The colon (:) separates the instruction address from the operation code. This punctuation always remains the same, and it informs the assembler that the instruction address has ended and the operation code begun. The memory address is terminated by a period. Several positions are left for the programmer's remarks, but the assembler does nothing with these. They are simply printed out for the programmer's own use.

Forms are usually provided for the programmer to write his program. (See Figure 43.) Note that the boundaries for each type of information are clearly shown. In general,

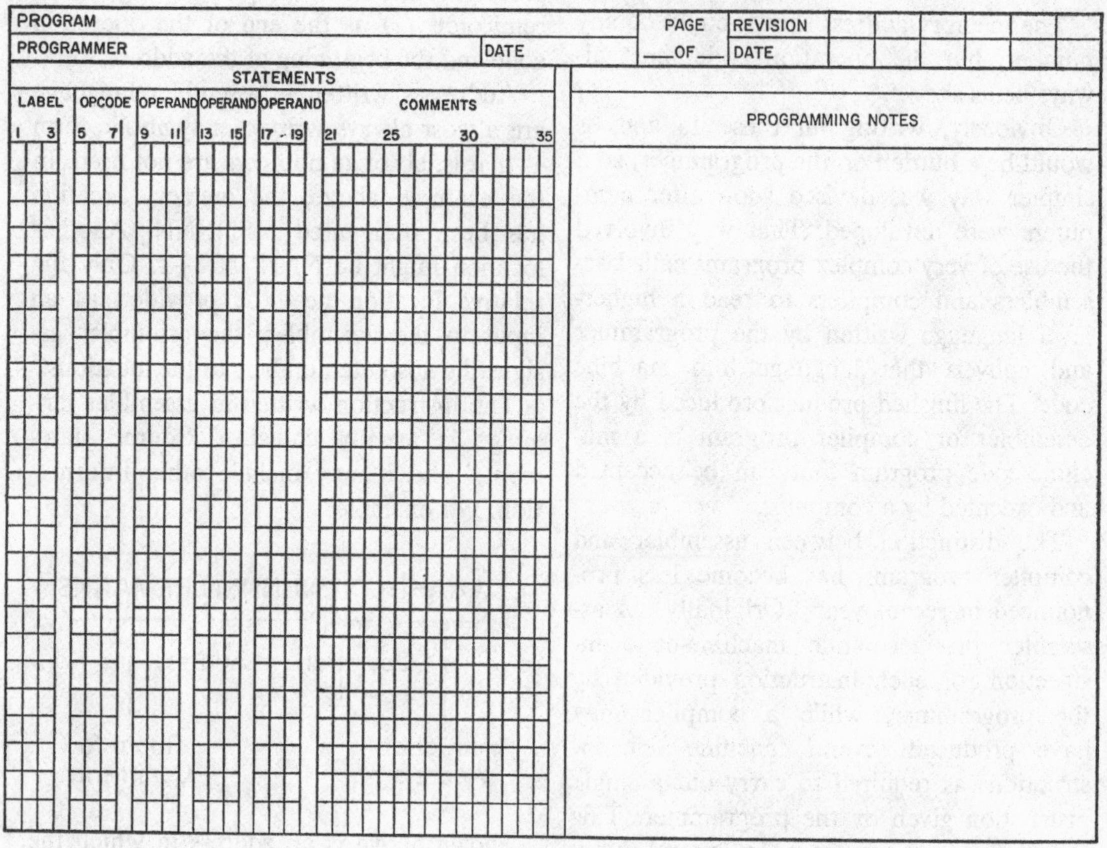

Figure 43. An Example of a Programmer's Coding Form

each section of the source statement is called a field (the instruction address field, operation code field, etc.). When the assembly process is completed, a program called the "object" is produced by the assembler. It is held in some form of permanent storage, such as cards or magnetic tape. Of course, it is in machine code but, to assist the programmer, the assembler prepares a printout in an easy-to-read form.

THE ASSEMBLY PROCESS

Assume for the purpose of this explanation that the programmer is going to use punched cards to hold his source statements for the assembly process. The process then begins when the programmer gives his coding form, which may be many pages in length, to a keypunch operator. Each source statement is punched into a card. Of course, a code that the computer recognizes is used. A card for the source statement used earlier as an example would appear as shown in Figure 44.

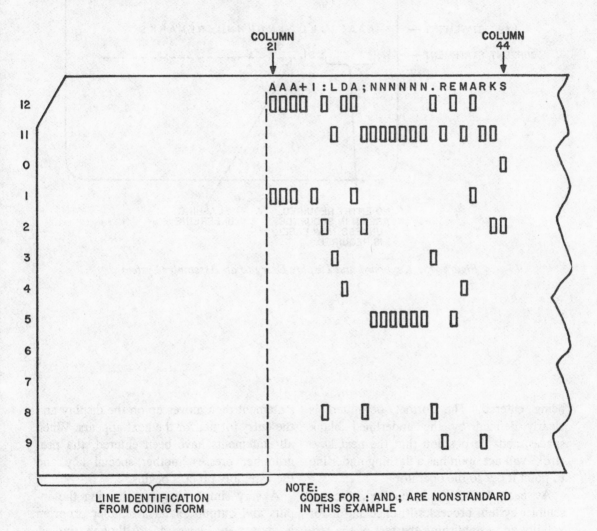

Figure 44. Format of a Card Holding One Source Statement

Some form of line identification from the coding form is used in the first twenty columns so that the cards can be placed in order. Then comes the single-line source statement.

A newer assembler system, designed to eliminate the punched-card phase and possibly even the coding-form phase for short programs prepared by experienced programmers, would present the coding-form format on a display and allow direct entry. An example of such a display appears in Figure 45.

Note that there are two source statements shown in the display, the first having been entered and the second in the process of

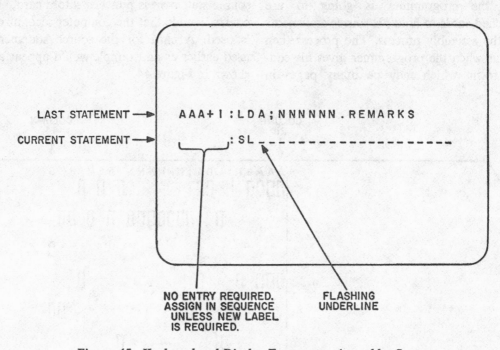

LAST STATEMENT ──▶ A A A + I : L D A ; N N N N N N . R E M A R K S

CURRENT STATEMENT ──▶   : S L _

NO ENTRY REQUIRED.
ASSIGN IN SEQUENCE
UNLESS NEW LABEL
IS REQUIRED.

FLASHING
UNDERLINE

Figure 45. Keyboard and Display Entry to an Assembler System

being entered. The format permitted is clearly defined by the underlined blank spaces, and the position that the next keystroke will act upon has a flashing underline to point it out to the operator.

As each keystroke is entered, the assembler system processes it, checking it for validity and establishing the rest of the format based upon the character entered. This system is far superior to the card entry system because some errors can be eliminated while the source statement is being typed. After the operator is satisfied that the statement is correct, he releases it to the assembler by pressing a certain key. This

statement then moves up on the display and the entry format for the next appears. When all statements have been entered, the programmer presses another special key and the assembly process begins.

A very simple diagram showing the inputs and outputs of an assembler program is shown in Figure 46. Although the assembler is shown as a single block here, it is usually broken down into a number of programs, one of which performs each function in the assembly process. For example, the tape on which the object program is recorded would be produced by a program entitled "object tape generator."

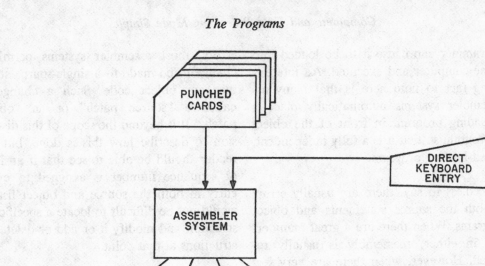

Figure 46. Inputs and Outputs of an Assembler System

The steps involved in the assembly process are as follows:

a. First, the entire card deck (or all the statements from the display and keyboard combination) are accepted by the assembler program, usually by a section of the assembler such as "source entry."

b. Each source statement is checked for entry errors. (Are the number of characters in the operation code field correct? Are the characters valid? Are addresses stated in one of the acceptable ways?)

c. Each source statement is then assigned an item number in the sequence in which it was entered.

d. A source-statement tape is then recorded. This can be used later in the assembly process.

e. At this point, the assembler usually informs the operator of the number of errors encountered and provides a source-statement listing for the programmer.

f. After the errors are corrected by the programmer, the assembler converts each source statement into machine code and records it on the object tape. Both recording of the tape and printing of any object listing are usually done under manual control—that is, the operator is given a choice of what is to be done, and when.

g. When satisfied that the object tape holds the program as he wants it, the programmer can cause it to be loaded into the computer and executed. An interesting fact to note here is that many assembler systems automatically place a loading program in front of the object program so that it is a fully independent, self-loading program.

Needless to say, there are usually errors in both the source statements and object programs. When there are a great many errors in either, reassembly is usually required. However, when there are very few errors, most assembler systems permit a change to be made to a single-source statement or object code. Such a change is called a "source patch" or an "object patch." It is beyond the scope of this discussion to describe how this is done, but the reader should be able to see that if an item or sequence number is assigned to every entry in both the source and object lists it would not be difficult to locate a specific instruction and modify it or add or delete instructions at that point.

HOW A PROGRAM IS ORGANIZED

Regardless of the reason for writing a program, someone must have stated the program's purpose and objectives. This is done in a broad statement of *program requirements*.

Next comes a detailed definition of the functions that the program is to perform, including such things as input and output formats, rates at which data are to be handled, equipment required, etc. This definition is usually given in a document called a *program specification*.

Once the overall approach to meeting the goals set forth in the program specification is decided upon, the program is usually divided into several clear-cut functions to be performed. Depending upon the complexity, one or many programmers may be involved in the programming task.

At this point, a brief description of the levels of program organization is desirable. The following are given in order of size:

a. A subroutine is the smallest group of instructions considered as a unit. It always has at least one specific function to perform, but this function must be combined with others to be of value.

b. Next in order of size and complexity comes a "routine." This is a fairly large number of instructions, perhaps one hundred or more, that are considered as a unit and perform one specific function. Again, a routine, like a subroutine, is not capable of standing alone. It must be combined with others to be of value. For example, a routine may require that its inputs be established before the routine starts.

c. A "program" is next. It generally consists of a large number of instructions and is made up of several routines. A "program" is intended to perform a specific function from beginning to end —in other words, it can stand alone. The "object tape generator" referred to in the assembly-process description is an example of what would be called a "program."

d. The largest group is called an "operating system," usually shortened to "system." It consists of at least several programs, which are called upon one at a time as the need arises. One of the programs in an operating system is usually an "executive," the function of which is to determine what the current requirements are and to call in the program or programs necessary to meet them. The group of programs that make up the assembler is an example of an operating system.

Flow-chart Symbols

Assume for the purposes of this discussion that a large "routine" is to be prepared by a programmer. He organizes the routine by a technique called "flow charting." A flow chart is simply a group of symbols that represents the processes, inputs, outputs, and decisions involved in reaching the objectives of the routine. Once a routine is organized into a flow chart, the programmer begins by writing the instructions necessary to meet the requirements of each block in the flow chart.

Symbols used in flow charts vary somewhat from one computer company to the next, but there has been some attempt at standardization. The most common symbols are shown in Figure 47 and described below.

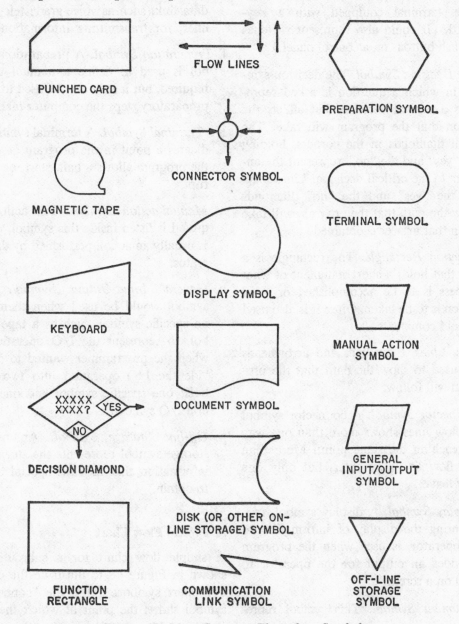

FLOW LINES

PUNCHED CARD

PREPARATION SYMBOL

CONNECTOR SYMBOL

MAGNETIC TAPE

TERMINAL SYMBOL

DISPLAY SYMBOL

KEYBOARD

MANUAL ACTION SYMBOL

XXXXX XXXX? YES

NO

DECISION DIAMOND

DOCUMENT SYMBOL

GENERAL INPUT/OUTPUT SYMBOL

FUNCTION RECTANGLE

DISK (OR OTHER ON-LINE STORAGE) SYMBOL

COMMUNICATION LINK SYMBOL

OFF-LINE STORAGE SYMBOL

Figure 47. Most Common Flow-chart Symbols

a. *Punched-card Symbol.* The punched-card symbol is used to represent either inputs from cards or an output to be punched into cards.

b. *Magnetic-tape Symbol.* The magnetic-tape symbol represents either an input from magnetic tape or an output to magnetic tape.

c. *Keyboard Symbol.* The keyboard symbol represents a manual input from a typewriter linked to the computer or computer terminal equipped with a keyboard. (It could also represent switches or push buttons on a control panel.)

d. *The Decision Symbol.* The decision symbol in which a question is asked represents a critical decision that affects the action that the program will take. The small diamonds in the corners, holding the "yes" and the "no," represent the answers to the critical decision. Lines leaving the "yes" and the "no" diamonds show the path that the program will take when that answer is obtained.

e. *Function Rectangle.* The rectangle is a box that holds a short statement of what process is to be accomplished or what action is to be taken. Often it is also used to hold comments.

f. *Flow Lines.* Flow lines and arrowheads are used to show the path that the program will follow.

g. *Connector Symbol.* A connector symbol for flow lines shows more than one way of reaching the same point. More than one flow line may enter, but only one may leave.

h. *Display Symbol.* A display symbol, representing the display of information to an operator, is used when the program provides an output for the operator to read on a screen.

i. *Document Symbol.* This symbol represents either an input or an output. An input might be an order form to be entered at the keyboard by an operator. An output might be a printed report at a printer.

j. *Disk and Other On-line Storage Symbol.* This symbol represents either an input from or an output to a magnetic disk or other types of on-line storage devices.

k. *Communications-link Symbol.* A communications-link symbol represents a data link, such as voice-grade telephone lines, for transmitting information.

l. *Preparation Symbol.* A preparation symbol is used to define a manual action required, but it may also be used to show preparatory steps the computer takes.

m. *Terminal Symbol.* A terminal symbol indicates a point in the program at which the program allows a halt, start, or interrupt.

n. *Manual-action Symbol.* The action required is listed inside this symbol, and it is usually an action performed by the operator.

o. *General Input-Output Symbol.* This symbol would be used when there was no specific symbol, such as a tape symbol, to represent the I/O operation or when the programmer wanted to subdivide the I/O operation into two symbols: one specific symbol and one general I/O symbol.

p. *Off-line Storage Symbol.* An off-line storage symbol represents the storage of information that requires special action to obtain.

A Typical Flow Chart

A simple flow chart for a subroutine is shown in Figure 48 to illustrate the use of flow-chart symbols. First, the "connector" symbol shows the point at which the subroutine can be entered. This symbol would be given a symbolic name so that any other part of the program could enter this subroutine by simply stating its name to the assembler program. Assume, for this example, that the subroutine is called "SORT." The word "SORT" would be placed in the label (the instruction address field) when the subroutine is originally entered in source-statement form.

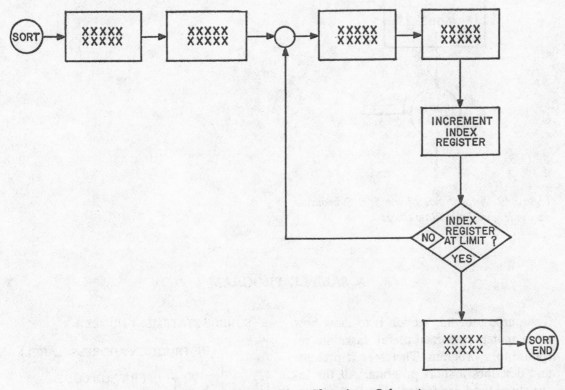

Figure 48. Example of a Flow Chart for a Subroutine

Next come two rectangles in which functions to be performed are stated. The programmer would write the instructions necessary to perform these functions in assembler language and enter them in a coding form. A connector symbol then shows that the next rectangle can be entered from either of two ways: (1) from the initial steps, or (2) from the repetitive steps as represented by the output of the decision diamond.

The next three rectangles show additional functions to be performed, the last of which is to increment an index register each time this group of functions is performed.

Next, the decision-diamond symbol shows the contents of the index register being tested. The test is, "Is the index register equal to the limit?" If the limit has not been reached, the subroutine is to continue. When the limit is reached, however, results are to be stored and the subroutine ended.

The "stop" could be represented by either a terminal or a connector symbol, depending upon how this subroutine was linked to others. Assume that a connector symbol was used. In this case, it could be assigned a symbolic name, perhaps SORT END, and other programs could then be linked to the

SORT END by the assembler. On the next higher-level flow chart, the sort subroutine illustrated would be a single rectangle like that shown in Figure 49.

In summary: Flow charts are used at all levels of program organization, from subroutines to operating systems, to define the functions to be performed and to place them in logical order.

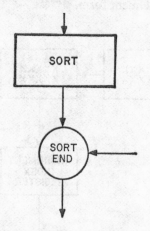

Figure 49. Appearance of the Sort Subroutine on the Higher-level Flow Chart

A SAMPLE PROGRAM

The purpose of this section is to show how a computer performs useful tasks in response to a program. Therefore it presents and describes a short program. All the instructions used are from the typical instruction set given in Unit 3, and the program is given in source statements using the assembler-language format shown earlier in this unit. The program is shown as it would appear on a coding form in Figure 50, and the flow chart for the program follows in Figure 51.

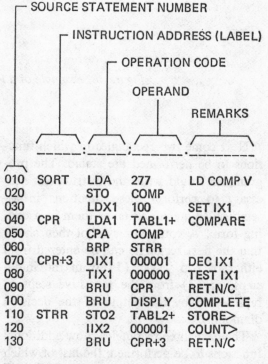

010	SORT	LDA	277	LD COMP V
020		STO	COMP	
030		LDX1	100	SET IX1
040	CPR	LDA1	TABL1+	COMPARE
050		CPA	COMP	
060		BRP	STRR	
070	CPR+3	DIX1	000001	DEC IX1
080		TIX1	000000	TEST IX1
090		BRU	CPR	RET.N/C
100		BRU	DISPLY	COMPLETE
110	STRR	STO2	TABL2+	STORE>
120		IIX2	000001	COUNT>
130		BRU	CPR+3	RET.N/C

Figure 50. The Sample Program on a Coding Form

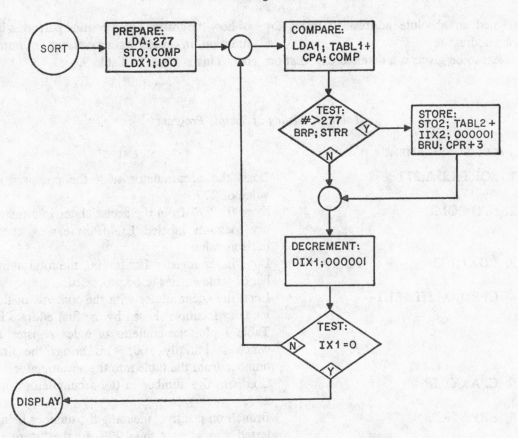

Figure 51. Flow Chart of the Sample Program

First, a summary of the purpose of the routine and how the steps in the flow chart reach its goals: The purpose of this routine is to sort through a table of 100 numbers and locate all those that are greater than 277. All numbers meeting this requirement are to be stored in another table for use by a display routine. The flow chart shows how this is accomplished. The source statements written in each block on the flow chart are not normally placed there by a programmer; they are included here to assist the reader in relating the chart symbols to the statements in the coding form.

The first rectangle in the chart shows preparation. Next, the actual comparison against 277 is made.

The first decision diamond then shows the results of the comparison being checked. When a number greater than 277

is found, it is stored and the comparison procedure is repeated for the next number.

After each number is tested, the second decision diamond checks to see if all 100 numbers have been processed. When they have, an entry to the display routine is made.

The address of the table of 100 numbers to be processed was assigned the symbolic address of TABL1 by the routine used to load the numbers in the table, so this program can use TABL1 as a starting address and be assured that the absolute address of the table will be put in during the assembly process.

The table in which all numbers greater than 277 will be stored is called TABL2, and the routine that will display these numbers will refer to TABL2 as an address with the assurance that the assembler will have assigned an absolute address to this symbolic address.

Next to be given is a detailed explanation of how the thirteen-step routine performs its function, in order by source-statement number. This is given in Table 3.

Table 3. Listing of Sample Program

SOURCE STATEMENT	MEANING
1. SORT:LDA;277	Load the accumulator with the comparison value of 277.
2. STO;COMP	Store the 277 from the accumulator in a memory location labeled COMP, meaning comparison value.
3. LDX1;100	Load index register 1 with 100, the total number of table entries to be processed.
4. CPR:LDA1;TABL1+	Load the accumulator with the contents of the memory location chosen by the first address in Table 1 plus the contents of index register 1, which is initially 100. This brings the first number from the table into the accumulator.
5. CPA;COMP	Compare the number in the accumulator with 277.
6. BRP;STRR	Branch on positive, meaning the number being tested was greater than 277, to the "store in Table 2 routine."
7. CPR+3:DIX1;000001	Decrement index register 1 by 1.
8. TIX1;000000	Test index register 1 for 0.
9. BRU;CPR	Return to decrement and test index register; then finish comparison if the index register is not equal to 0.
10. BRU;DISPLY	Branch to the display routine because index register 1 is 0, indicating that all 100 numbers in TABL1 have been processed.
11. STRR:STO2;TABL2+	Store the contents of the accumulator in Table 2, modified by the contents of index register 2, which is initially 0.
12. IIX2;000001	Increment index register 2.
13. BRU:CPR+3	Return to the comparison routine.

HIGH-LEVEL LANGUAGES

Programming a computer is a specialized and difficult task. When the number of computers in use was limited, the users maintained staffs of programmers who used a programming language similar to the assembler language described earlier. Each major function to be performed was broken down into assembler language steps and entered into the computer. The disadvantage of this of course was that it took a highly skilled person a long time to do.

It quickly became essential to make programming easier. This required that the gap between the computer and the user's statements of what must be done be bridged. In other words, the user should be able to tell the computer what to do in the user's own terms and frame of reference.

In order to achieve this objective, the computer industry began to offer programming languages that were much closer to English than to assembler language. Among some of the names that the reader may have heard are.

APL	Algorithmic Programming Language
COBOL	Common Business-oriented Language
BASIC	Beginner's All-purpose Symbolic Instruction Code
FORTRAN	Formula Translation
RPG	Report Program Generator

Many other less well-known languages are also available. In general, each computer builder offers at least one of these high-level languages that will operate on his line of equipment. The purpose of this description is to provide the reader with a general idea of what a high-level language looks like and how the computer handles it.

First of all, it should be kept in mind that a computer is limited by its basic machine-language instruction set. If the function stated cannot be performed by the machine-language instructions, it doesn't make any difference what the source language is. So the point is that all source statements must be converted to machine language regardless of the level of the programming language being used. For that reason, not all of these high-level languages can be used by all computers.

Each high-level language has an instruction set and source-statement formats, just like the assembler language shown earlier. Coding forms are usually provided to assist the programmer in using the language.

The conversion of high-level language source statements into a form used by the computer is done by complex compiler programs in a variety of ways. One feature that many have in common, however, is the instruction interpreter concept. This operates as follows: A programmer examines the function to be performed by an instruction in a higher-level language. He then determines several things, such as where the result is to be placed when the operation is completed. Is it to be placed in a memory location that has been assigned a symbolic address? If so, where will the absolute address be defined?

Once the programmer has determined this type of information, he knows what machine-language instructions will be required to perform the intent of the high-level instruction and how the links to other high-level instructions are to be established.

The next step is to write the machine-language routine and test it. Of course, this is done in assembler language. This routine is now an "instruction interpreter" for one high-level instruction.

Examine first a high-level instruction for which an interpreter is to be written. Assume for the purpose of this description that the language is called simply commerce language (CL). The instruction to be examined is:

TRI—Translate Input
Operation Code 370

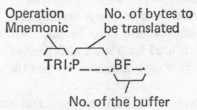

Operation Mnemonic   No. of bytes to be translated

TRI;P____,BF_.

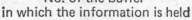

No. of the buffer
in which the information is held

This instruction translates the contents of the buffer (BF) specified from EBCDIC to ASCII (which are both codes used within the computer). The number of entries in the buffer is specified by the digits following "P" in P——— —.

An example of use is as follows:

TRI;P256,BF1.

Assume that a 256-byte record has been read from a magnetic tape and placed in buffer 1. However, the tape was provided from a communications system that transmitted and recorded in EBCDIC, and our system, which displays characters chosen by an ASCII code, cannot use EBCDIC directly. One instruction in commerce language can accomplish the translation required.

After examining the translation and linking requirements of the TRI instruction, the programmer prepares an instruction interpreter routine in assembler language and has it converted to machine language by an assembler system. He then "tags," or labels, the routine somehow.

In the case of the TRI instruction the interpreter requires 190 machine-language instructions. The programmer then prepares interpreters for each of the other instructions in commerce language, perhaps 75 interpreters in all, averaging 200 machine-language instructions each.

The next step is for the user to write his application program in CL. This is done, and the program is supplied (from a coding form) to the commerce language assembler. The CL assembler performs some of the functions of the assembler discussed earlier in this unit, *but it does not convert CL source statements to machine language.* It assigns an operation code to each instruction, 370 is used for TRI, and organizes the rest of each source statement so that the instruction interpreter can use it.

Assume that for TRI the operation code of 370 is placed in one memory location

and the P and BF fields are placed in the second. Also assume for purposes of this explanation that all instructions in CL are handled in this manner. Refer to Figure 52 for an example of how this would be organized in memory.

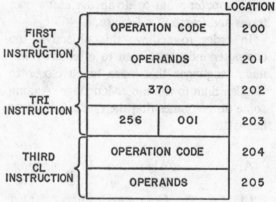

Figure 52. Organization of High-level Language Instructions in Memory

After assembling his CL program, the user is ready to execute it. He then loads the assembled CL program. Placed at the beginning of the CL program by the assembler is a supervisor program whose function is to read each CL instruction from memory and then locate and execute the interpreter for that instruction. Although there are many ways in which this could be done, the following is used to illustrate the principles involved.

The supervisor includes a routine called RNI—Read Next Instruction, meaning "read the next CL instruction from memory." It reads the contents of the two memory locations in which TRI was placed by the CL assembler. Then it uses the operation code of 370 as a memory address in a Stack and Branch instruction. When the Stack and Branch to address 370 is executed, the TRI instruction interpreter is found because the first machine-language instruction of the interpreter was placed in location 370 by the CL assembler.

The 190 machine-language instructions of the TRI instruction interpreter are then executed to carry out the intent of the TRI instruction, and the last instruction of the interpreter is Exit. This causes a return to the supervisor's RNI routine. It reads the next CL instruction from memory and performs a Stack and Branch instruction to its interpreter. Again, the interpreter ends with an Exit instruction to return to the RNI routine. This continues until the commerce language program is complete.

OTHER PROGRAMMING TERMS IN GENERAL USE

This section is devoted to some specialized terms used in programming which, although they are not directly related to one another, are grouped and explained here for convenience.

The first programming term, "pseudo instruction," is related to an assembler system. Like the other source statements described earlier in this unit, pseudo instructions are inputs to an assembler system; however, they are *not converted directly into machine-code instructions*.

Assume that there was a pseudo instruction called "ASN-Assign." This statement could be used to assign an absolute number to a symbolic starting address for the object program, as follows: ASN:BBB;7502. ASN tells the assembler that the address given as BBB is to be absolute address 7502 in memory and that this is where the object program is to be located. Note that while this pseudo instruction has a very significant effect on the generation of the object program by the assembler system, it does not become part of the object program itself.

Another pseudo instruction might be "TTL-Title," meaning to instruct the assembler system to place a title at the top of a page of a source listing. When the assembler read such a pseudo instruction, it would advance the printer paper to the top of a form and type the heading given in this instruction. Note that the pseudo instruction again has a significant effect but is not made part of the object program.

Next to be discussed is the term "macro instruction." Somewhat similar to a pseudo instruction in that it is not converted directly to machine language, a macro instruction is one that requires a large number of machine instructions to execute. It may even require several routines. Although the instructions in the higher-level languages are essentially macro instructions by the foregoing definitions, macro instructions are usually thought of as being even larger in scope. For example, an INITIALIZE statement might be considered a macro instruction. Upon receiving such a command, the executive program in an operating system would clear all interfaces with peripheral equipment, bring all tapes to load point, bring all other peripheral equipment to a ready state, and branch to the first program in the operating system.

Opposite of macro, which means very large, is micro, meaning very small. Micro programming is usually thought of as making selections within a machine instruction.

In all computers, each instruction is carried out by a series of individual steps. For example, a simple CAD-Clear and Add instruction, which reads the contents of a memory location, clears the accumulator and adds the contents of the subject memory location to the now cleared accumulator, would be carried out by the following steps:

a. Place the memory address in the memory address register.
b. Read memory.

c. Transfer the memory data to the A register.
d. Clear the accumulator.
e. Add the A register and accumulator.
f. Transfer the sum to the accumulator.

If the computer was designed so that changes within this instruction could be made for specific applications of the machine, then making these changes would be micro programming. This is not usually done by the applications programmer.

"Firmware," meaning an intermediate stage between "hardware," the equipment itself, which is not changeable, and "software," meaning programs, which are very quickly and easily changed, is another term that needs definition. It is commonly used to mean a group of instructions permanently or semipermanently stored in a special memory called a ROM (read-only memory). This program is prepared when the computer is designed and it is usually intended to perform a fixed function, although it is often the case that the ROM can be replaced with one holding a different program. For example, when the "LOAD FROM TAPE" push button is depressed on the control panel of a large computer, it causes a program stored in a ROM to be executed. This performs the functions necessary to read the program to be performed from magnetic tape. It starts the tape, reads at least one record, and causes the computer to accept the record as a program and execute it.

The next subject to be discussed is the terms used to describe types of programs. Essentially there are only three types of programs:

a. Applications programs, the purpose of which is to use the computer to perform some useful job—to "apply" the computer, in other words.
b. Diagnostic programs, the purpose of which is to test the computer's ability to perform its intended function. These programs are usually performed when some type of trouble has arisen, although they are also used to test the system's readiness.
c. Programming systems, which include the assemblers, compilers, and all the aids necessary to convert the programmer's statements into both application and diagnostic programs.

Utility programs are considered to be a fourth type of program by some, but they are really a subdivision of the applications programs group. An example of a utility program is one used to copy files from one storage medium to another; from a disk to a magnetic tape is typical. This utility program is not used until the computer's primary program is finished preparing the disk file; then the utility makes a back-up copy on the file.

QUIZ ON THE SUBJECT MATTER IN UNIT 4

1. Define "programming."
2. What does machine code mean?
3. What is the purpose of assembler and compiler systems?
4. Is there any difference between an assembler and a compiler?
5. What is the purpose of the punctuation included in source statements?
6. How are memory addresses usually specified in source statements?
7. What is an object program?
8. How does the assembler/compiler system identify source statements?

9. What is the primary advantage that assembler/compiler systems that allow source-statement entry from a keyboard/display unit have over those that accept punched cards?

10. Why is a coding form used?

11. What are the four outputs normally available from an assembler system?

12. Arrange the following terms in order of size (starting with the smallest): operating system, subroutine, program, routine.

13. Why are flow charts necessary?

14. Why are "high level" languages necessary?

15. What is an instruction interpreter?

16. The last five questions in this quiz require the reader to perform some very simple programming exercises to develop additional knowledge of programming. Use the mnemonics given in the instruction set from Unit 3 and a form similar to that in the sample program. If necessary, simply write out a statement of what must be done—the purpose of these examples being to illustrate principles rather than to teach programming in a specific language.

Problem A

The computer is reading one record at a time from tape and looking for record number 050. (They are in sequential order.) The last record read is stored in memory, with the record number (which is the first byte in the record) held in the first location of a buffer area labeled RECIN. If the record just read is No. 50, the record is to be processed by a routine called SORT; if it is not No. 50, the next record is to be read by a routine called RETAPE. Test the record number and go to the proper routine after the test.

Problem B

Record No. 50 has now been located and is held in the memory buffer starting at location RECIN. This record is the payroll information for an employee, and we must determine whether or not a savings-bond deduction is to be made. Deductions are covered in byte 17 of the record, and savings bonds by bit 5 of byte 17. If bit 5 is a 1, a savings-bond deduction is to be made by a routine labeled SAVDED; if not, we are to test for United Fund deduction in a routine labeled TEFUND. Test the savings-bond bit and go to the proper routine.

Problem C

There are 100 employees in this company, so there are 100 records that must be processed. When each record is processed, index register 1 is incremented by 1. So after the last record is finished, the index register should contain 100. If it does, we are to go to a routine to calculate totals, called CALTOT; if it does not, we are to return to processing the next record, which begins with the RETAPE routine. Make the test for completion and go to the proper routine.

Problem D

Multiplication to arrive at the employee's Social Security deduction has taken place, and the results are held in the arithmetic unit. The most significant portion is to be placed in byte 15 of the employee's record and the least significant portion is to be placed in byte 16. Again, the employee's record is in memory, beginning at location RECIN. Store his Social Security deduction in the proper positions.

Problem E

Another updating of the employee's records is to be done. With this payroll period, he has chosen to participate in the retirement plan and have a deduction made from his pay. Recall from Problem B that the deduction types are recorded in byte 17. Bit 2 of this byte represents participation in the retirement plan. Located in memory are mask bytes to add deductions. The one to add retirement is in a location labeled +RETMK. Update byte 17 and return it to the proper location in memory.

UNIT 5

THE SYSTEMS

This unit describes computer "systems," meaning the combination of equipment and programs applied to a specific task. First we will discuss how a computer system comes into being.

To begin, a system analyst, who is an individual with broad experience in computer systems, studies the job requirements to determine what the computer and supporting equipment must do. This service is usually provided by a firm in the business of selling computers or programs, but many large companies and government agencies employ their own system analysts.

Factors that must be considered during system analysis include: the speed at which the data processing must be accomplished, total storage requirements, the need for communication with remote locations, space available, input and output media, compatibility with existing systems and processes, funds available for the new system, and personnel available to operate the system. These are only representative examples, of course, but they serve to point out that choosing a computer system is a task that must be done very carefully.

A second level of planning is then required for large systems, and this brings in engineering personnel. Floor plans, cooling requirements, and power requirements are established. Capacity of the computing equipment and programs available to meet the requirements laid out by the system analyst are evaluated. Equipment and programs are chosen, and any customization of existing products or preparation of new products for the proposed system are decided upon. Close co-ordination with the system analyst and, in turn, the intended user is required during this planning. When this second stage is complete, the system exists "on paper."

The last stage of preparation involves three levels of personnel: the system analyst, engineers, and the technicians responsible for installation and testing of both the equipment and the programs. After technicians install the equipment, a series of diagnostic programs is run in order to verify that the equipment is operating properly. Then the applications programs prepared for this installation are tested with the customer's data and jobs to determine that they are operating properly. Finally, the overall system is operated under normal conditions to see that it meets the original requirements established. It is common to provide a trial period during which the customer continues processing his data in both the old way and with the new system to determine that the new installation is providing the desired results under all conditions. During this time, training of customer personnel takes place, operating procedures are developed, and the remaining problems are solved.

As a last step, the system is turned over to the customer. This usually involves a formalized acceptance procedure during which the customer acknowledges that the system does meet the requirements established in the original agreement. When the system is complete, it would resemble the example of the typical computer installation described in this unit.

AN EXAMPLE OF A COMPUTER INSTALLATION

A sketch of a typical computer room using a medium-size computer with considerable peripheral equipment appears in Figure 53. Then, in Figure 54, which follows, a block diagram showing the data flow between these units and between this installation and others appears.

Notice in the sketch that the floor space is completely open between units, and is not cluttered with cables. This is because all cables interconnecting the units are run under the floor, and they enter the cabinets near the bottom. An alternative is a false ceiling from which the cables descend through ducts to enter the cabinet tops.

The installation shown could be that used in a bank. Communications controllers play an important role in this installation because it is necessary to communicate with many display and keyboard terminals at bank branches. A bank teller may make an inquiry regarding the state of a customer's account over these communication lines. In addition, deposits and withdrawals conducted at the branches can be transferred over telephone lines to the computer in the central bank.

The physical arrangement of the equipment in the room is closely related to its function. Begin by considering the place of the operator's console, which is a low unit over which a seated operator can see all other units in the room. From the operator's console, the user directs the loading of programs and the data to be processed.

Six tape units are required because of the massive records that must be kept by the bank. Each is a stand-alone upright unit. At the top of each is a large address label, usually housed in an easily changed thumbwheel. This allows the console operator to read at a glance the current address of each tape unit. Of course, the operator can also view the front panels of the tape drives to determine if they are loaded and ready.

Two large disk drives are also provided. They hold the information used frequently. Although these units generally do not have address indicators, the operator can view them being loaded and determine when they are ready.

Immediately behind the operator are the card reader and printer. Tapes are generally the source of operating programs, but backup copies might be provided on cards.

The printer may be a low-volume unit intended to support only the daily activities, or it might be a very high-volume unit used to print all customer transactions, such as checking-account statements. In general, a high-volume printer would be located separately, in an area where its output could be handled without interfering with activities in the computer room.

The central processor unit, which includes the memory, arithmetic, and control units of a general-purpose computer, stands at the left side of the room. It is unattended, and even power is applied by pushing a switch on the operator's console.

Both the input/output controller and the communications controller are also large, unattended units. Near the communications controller are telephone data sets—that is, telephones equipped to exchange data with the branch banks. They are equipped to call and answer automatically, but this can be overridden by manual intervention so that voice communications can be established.

Located at each branch bank are one or more remote terminals, each consisting of a display and keyboard combination necessary for the operator to ask questions of the main computer and read the answers supplied, or to enter transaction information and view its acceptance by the main com-

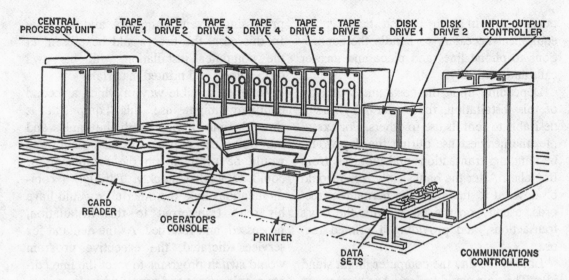

Figure 53. Layout of a Typical Computer Room

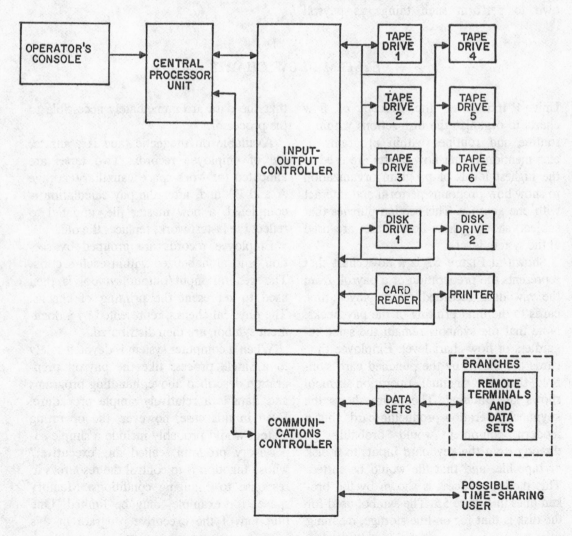

Figure 54. Block Diagram of a Typical Computer System

puter. Also in each branch bank is the equipment necessary to handle the connections to phone lines and place and answer calls automatically.

Depending upon the costs and workload of this installation, the owner may find it desirable to rent its use to others. For example, the heaviest use during the day would be handling transactions and inquiries from branches. After the banks close, time would be devoted to updating the permanent records, usually on the tapes, with the day's transactions, and providing a printed record.

Late in the day the computer might stand idle. The time could be leased to a company with no data-processing equipment of its own to perform such things as payroll processing, inventory control, and ordering. In this case, the user would be present at the computer installation with his own disks, tapes, and printed materials.

Another possible way in which a second company might use this equipment is through time sharing. Both the bank's and the other users' programs and data base would be available on the equipment, or could be loaded quickly. Through a communications link, the other user would have his data transferred to this installation, processed, and returned. As the demand for services dictated, the executive program would switch programs to meet the immediate requirements and return when they were satisfied.

SYSTEM FLOW CHARTS

Unit 4 introduced the concept of flow charts to organize the instructions within a routine and routines within programs. It also mentioned that flow charts are used at the highest levels of program organization to show how programs perform and interact with one another. This section pursues that subject, showing how flow charts are used at the system level.

Shown in Figure 55 is a flow chart that represents the preparation of a payroll from the raw data recorded on employee time cards to the final printing of the paychecks. Note that the symbols remain the same regardless of flow-chart level. Employee time cards are shown by the punched card symbol; then the manual operation symbol shows keypunching. The figure shows the keypunch operation producing cards, but a modern computer would probably go directly from the keyboard inputs to a disk or tape file, and that file would be sorted. This modern process is shown by the broken lines in Figure 55. The symbol used for the disk is that for on-line storage, meaning that the data are immediately accessible to the processor.

Available on magnetic tape is a master file of employee records. Two tapes are allocated for work space (auxiliary storage A and B) and, after the pay calculation is completed, a new master file, updated to reflect the lastest work, replaces the old.

Employee records are grouped by section, and alphabetized within each section. The general input/output symbol is then used to represent the printing of checks. The physical checks, represented by a document symbol, are then distributed.

When a computer system is devoted solely to a single process like the payroll preparation described above, handling programs and data is a relatively simple procedure. Even in this case, however, the operating system would probably include a simple supervisory program, called an "executive," whose function is to control the resources in response to changing conditions. Memory space, for example, may be limited. One function of the executive program in this

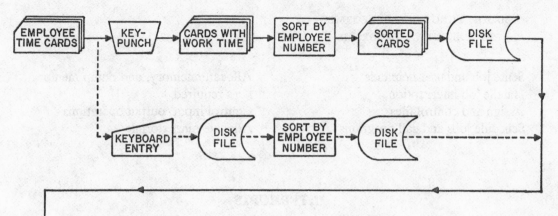

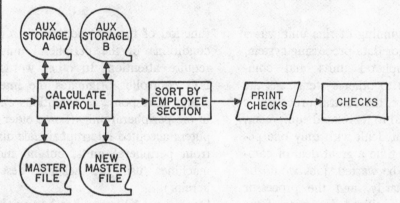

Figure 55. Example of a System Flow Chart

case would be to acquire one processing program at a time, load it into memory, and describe the location of the data to be processed to the processing program. The description would be in the form of a file name and the number of the unit in which the file was stored. When the first processing program is completed, it so informs the executive and the executive acquires, or "calls," the next program to be performed. "Calling" a program is the most common term used to describe the acquisition of a program or data file by the executive.

Listed below are some of the functions performed by an executive program. First, there is always an "interrupt handler" routine in the executive. The interrupts to which this routine responds may be the "hardware interrupts," like those described later in this unit, or a "software interrupt," meaning some action taken by the program

in progress to get the attention of the executive.

In response to the new conditions, the executive may be called upon to immediately remove and record the contents of memory. This is called a "memory dump." In this case, the contents of memory are moved to one of the mass-storage devices. Of course, the executive has maintained a record of how much mass-storage space is available, and where it is located. After moving the memory contents, the executive establishes a record of existing conditions, for recovery purposes, and "calls" whatever new programs are required. Additional detail on executives could only be provided if a specific operating system were to be discussed, but the reader should be aware that the seven basic functions listed are usually required by all operating systems.

MAJOR FUNCTIONS PERFORMED
BY EXECUTIVE PROGRAMS

Sense job and user demands	Allocate memory, and dump memory
Handle job interruption	as required
Assign and control files	Control input/output operations
Schedule jobs and call programs	Allocate mass storage

INTERRUPTS

Shown at the beginning of this unit was a diagram of a major data-processing system, with many peripheral units and communications lines to other systems. As the reader now knows, the central processor is very fast compared to its related equipment, so if the processor dealt with only one peripheral unit at a time a great deal of computer time could be wasted, jobs would be delayed unnecessarily, and the processor would not be fully utilized. However, if the processor tried to operate several peripheral units at once and still perform its internal processing work, the programmer would be confronted with a nearly impossible task of keeping the jobs and data in order. Nearly all computers now have built into them a scheme by which a peripheral unit can notify the processor at critical points, such as completion of a job or when an error occurs. This notification is called an interrupt. In addition, the interrupts are each assigned a place in a priority network. How these operate is the subject of this section.

First, it is necessary to briefly review the processor's relationship with peripheral units. There are three points to be made:

a. The computer's input/output unit includes I/O controllers to adapt the computer to speed, data form, and mechanical features of the peripheral unit.
b. All connections between the peripheral unit and the computer are made through the respective I/O controller, so it is a function of the I/O controller to detect conditions in the peripheral unit that require attention. In other words, the I/O controller originates the interrupt signal in response to conditions existing in the peripheral unit. (Some older computers accepted interrupt signals directly from peripheral units, but all modern machines use the scheme described herein.)
c. Once the I/O controller has originated an interrupt signal in response to conditions in its related peripheral unit, *the interrupt is forwarded to the control unit for action*. Only the control unit can cause the processor to change its operation.

In the large system shown, one would expect to find interrupts like the following:

a. From the disk controller—
1. Reading or writing complete
2. Selected unit and address located
3. Error condition

b. From the magnetic tape controller—
1. Motion command (rewind, backspace, etc.) complete
2. Reading or writing complete
3. Error condition

c. From the printer—
1. Motion command (carriage return, line feed, etc.) complete
2. Printing complete
3. Error condition

d. From the keyboards—
 1. Input completed
 2. Error condition

e. From the displays—
 1. Computer input accepted (display is complete)
 2. Error condition

f. From the communications units—
 1. Message ready for computer
 2. Message accepted by remote unit
 3. Error condition

The next thing that must be considered is the priority assigned to each of the interrupts; this is usually based upon the characteristics of the peripheral unit. Some units make it impossible to recover the information if they are not given immediate attention, while others offer the opportunity to recover even if an interrupt is ignored. The characteristics of the respective units are discussed in the following paragraphs.

First to be examined are the communications units. Assume that this computer is receiving a long-distance data transfer over voice-grade telephone lines from a remote site. The rate of transfer is *very slow* compared to computer speed, but the message is being sent in "real time"— that is, it is happening right now, and the communications controller has storage capacity for only one character at a time. If a character is not accepted within a short time, it could be overrun by the next and, of course, would be lost. This makes it necessary for the computer to give a "communications interrupt" the highest priority.

Next in the priority scheme might come the keyboard inputs. Here, an operator is typing information, again in "real time." If a stroke is not accepted within a reasonable time, it is overrun by the next stroke. Of course, a large buffer could be placed in the I/O controller to overcome this, but in many cases the computer may be waiting for a keystroke to control its operation. So

it is important that keystrokes be accepted quickly.

The disk might come next in the priority scheme. It moves fairly rapidly. If the I/O controller cannot gain access to memory to transfer the data called for, the disk may physically pass the recording point. So it is important that the disk be given memory access quickly.

Tapes are somewhat slower than disks, but tapes too have the recording medium in motion, and their I/O controller must gain memory access to transfer data.

Printers and displays are usually lowest in the interrupt priority scheme. Most often each has a buffer capable of holding at least one line, and printers do not progress to the next line without instructions, so printers and displays can wait until the computer has time to service them.

There is one other possible source of an interrupt not yet discussed—that is an interrupt switch on the computer control panel. It is difficult to place the priority of this interrupt in the priority scheme because it varies so much from one computer to another. In addition, it is not used in normal operation but rather in equipment and program tests. The effect of the switch depends upon the program being used, but it almost always produces a very significant effect, such as stopping the program or skipping to another program. For purposes of this description, we will give the program-interrupt switch the highest priority in the interrupt scheme, assuming that it would not be used except under the conditions cited above.

This then leads us to the following order of priorities:

a. Program-interrupt switch
b. Communications interrupt
c. Keyboard interrupt
d. Disk interrupt
e. Tape interrupt

f. Printer interrupt
g. Display interrupt

Each of these interrupts is sent to a respective bi-stable device in the control unit. They are then summarized and the control unit is told that there either is or is not an interrupt condition existing.

At the end of each machine instruction the control unit checks the status of the interrupts, although there are some operations so important that the control unit can be set so as to ignore all interrupts. Each time the control unit finds an interrupt condition, it must determine its priority. Assuming that the control unit is not already responding to an interrupt condition, there is no conflict; the control unit simply determines where the interrupt originated and proceeds to branch to a routine needed to "service" that condition. When the servicing routine is completed, the control unit branches back to the point of interruption and continues where it left off. (It normally stores all the conditions necessary to recover.)

A conflict does arise, however, if the control unit is already engaged in an interrupt servicing routine when another occurs. At this point, the priority scheme goes into effect. Assume, for example, that a tape-interrupt servicing routine was being executed when a communications interrupt arrived. At the end of the current machine instruction, the control unit would switch to the communications-interrupt servicing routine, storing the conditions necessary to return. After servicing communications, it would then return to the tape servicing and, after completing that, it would return to normal operation.

It should be noted here that interrupt servicing routines are rather short. They usually perform only the tasks essential to avoiding problems, store the facts regarding the interrupt condition, and allow the normal programs to handle the data processing. An example of this is the communications-interrupt routine. Its purpose is to avoid loss of data due to an overrun or error, *not to process the incoming message*. It accepts the incoming character and stores it. Only when the message is completed is the message-processing program called in and executed.

COMMUNICATIONS BETWEEN SYSTEMS

The important role played by long-distance communications in the data-processing industry was shown in the computer system at the beginning of this unit, and communications will become even more important in the future as computing services are offered directly to the home. Therefore, this section describes some of the basic principles involved in the transfer of computer data over the most common communications lines of all, voice-grade telephone lines.

Telephone lines link most homes and businesses in the country. Although the telephone usually handles voice communications, the standard telephone lines can be used to transmit data. It should also be mentioned here that there are communication channels available that are intended solely for data transmission, and therefore they have a greater capability to transfer information than phone lines. However, the basic principles described here also apply to these special channels.

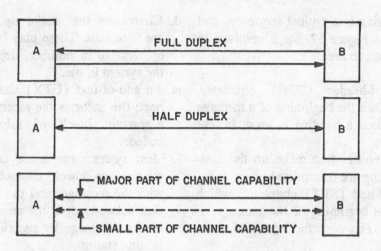

Figure 56. Communications Line Arrangements

There are three basic arrangements of communications lines between computing equipment, as shown in Figure 56. They are:

a. Full duplex, which provides two channels between units. In this case, a unit uses one line to send and the other to receive, and can be sending and receiving simultaneously.

b. Half duplex, which provides only one channel between units. This channel is bi-directional but can carry data in only one direction at any one time. Each time that a unit finishes sending and the other takes its turn sending, the line must be "turned around."

c. Reverse channel half duplex, which involves using most of the capability of a single channel for sending in one direction while the remainder is used as a low-speed "reverse" channel. In this case, the reverse channel can carry only a few bits per second and is used primarily for acknowledgments or sending error indications.

In the communications described in the following pages, binary data are sent from the transmitting unit to the receiving unit. A "mark" represents a 1 and a "space" represents a 0. This binary information is organized into groups of bits to form characters. Of course, the two units communicating with one another must be using the same code. (The transmission codes most commonly used are described in the next section.) In addition, the data sent must be organized according to specific rules, and it requires the use of predetermined control characters to co-ordinate the exchange of data; otherwise the receiving unit could not understand the message.

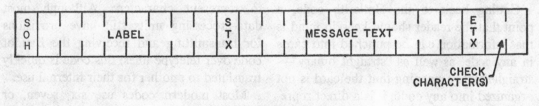

Figure 57. Typical Message Format

The following is a typical sequence, and it is shown in Figure 57. Steps involved in sending a message are:

a. A start-of-header (SOH) character, which defines the beginning of a message label, if such a heading is used, is sent first.

b. Then characters that make up the message heading are transmitted.

c. A start-of-text (STX) character, which defines the beginning of the message, is sent next. This ends the label and starts the text.

d. Characters that make up the message are then sent. These may be either fixed or variable in number, depending upon the system in use.

e. An end-of-text (ETX) character comes next; this informs the receiving unit that a certain block of information has ended.

f. Most systems use some error-detection scheme, so check characters are sent with the message, and the receiving station acknowledges the receipt of an error-free message by signaling the transmitting station.

COMMONLY USED CODES

Hollerith, BCD, EBCDIC, and ASCII are among the many codes used in the data-processing industry. A code is nothing more than specific arrangements of bits used to represent characters. An example of this is the Hollerith code, which is used in punched cards. Each column in the card is assigned to represent a character by punched holes in certain positions. A "D," for example, is represented by punched holes in rows 4 and 12 and the lack of holes in the remaining ten rows.

Any computer builder or user is able to design his own code for internal use, and many have done so. A problem of compatibility arises, however, when the data must be used by others. Translation from one code to another must be performed and, in some cases, this is a difficult and time-consuming process.

Getting back to the Hollerith code, a point that the reader should keep in mind is that information can be punched into cards in any code, as well as "straight binary"— straight binary meaning that the card is not organized into any code; it is a direct representation of binary information. This might be the case when an object program is punched into cards. The information in the cards is the machine code for instructions and addresses.

The Hollerith code does not make use of all possible combinations of the bit positions available in a column. This, and the fact that cards have many disadvantages (such as the large physical size required to store information), led to the development of more compact codes.

Another of the older codes is the Baudot code, which is a five-bit code used in teletypewriter equipment and is named after a French postal telegraph engineer. Five bits would normally provide the codes for only thirty-two characters but, by using upper- and lower-case shifting, this number can be doubled. By the time the function codes are subtracted from the sixty-four possible combinations, fifty-eight combinations are left to represent characters. Although most data-processing units still have provisions for transmitting and receiving the Baudot code over teletype lines, this code is quickly translated to another for their internal use.

Most modern codes use six, seven, or eight bits, closely matching the size of the byte, and standards have been established both in the United States and internationally. The two codes that the reader is likely to encounter most often are ASCII and EBCDIC, and these are discussed below. ASCII, meaning American Standard Code for Information Interchange, is a seven-bit code. It is also called USASCII, in which the USA simply means United States of America.

There are 128 combinations available in the ASCII set, numbered 000 through 177 octal, and the combinations for letters and numbers are shown in Table 4. Notice that the combinations for letters and numbers run in sequential order, which makes the code easier to use than the Hollerith and Baudot codes.

Table 4. ASCII and EBCDIC Codes (in Octal) for Numbers and Upper-case Letters

Character	ASCII	EBCDIC	Character	ASCII	EBCDIC
0	060	360	I	111	311
1	061	361	J	112	321
2	062	362	K	113	322
3	063	363	L	114	323
4	064	364	M	115	324
5	065	365	N	116	325
6	066	366	O	117	326
7	067	367	P	120	327
8	070	370	Q	121	330
9	071	371	R	122	331
A	101	301	S	123	342
B	102	302	T	124	343
C	103	303	U	125	344
D	104	304	V	126	345
E	105	305	W	127	346
F	106	306	X	130	347
G	107	307	Y	131	350
H	110	310	Z	132	351

EBCDIC means extended binary coded decimal interchange code, and this is an eight-bit code. BCD, binary coded decimal, was originally used in four-bit groups to represent numbers 0 through 9. It meant nothing more than that each four-bit group was to be read as a decimal digit. Next, six-bit BCD groups were used, and they included the alphabet. As the communication of data over long-distance lines developed, characters to control the communication

were needed, and this required the extension of BCD to EBCDIC. EBCDIC codes for numbers and upper-case letters are also shown in Table 4.

Up to this point we have discussed four codes that represent industry standards. A logical conclusion to this section then is to describe a less well-known code to illustrate the many other possibilities available to computer manufacturers. The code to be used in this example is an eight-bit code, the eight bits being read in octal for this discussion. It is called a "special" for this discussion and is constructed as follows:

Character	Code
Space (a blank)	000
+	001
-	002
0	003
1	004
2	005
3	006
4	007
5	010
6	011
7	012
8	013
9	014
A	015
B	016
≈	≈
Z	046

In this case, the computer manufacturer has chosen to begin his character set with space, +, and − to occupy the first three binary combinations available. Thereafter, each numeric character is represented by a binary combination which, if read in decimal, is a number that is three higher than the respective numeric character. Hence the name "excess 3" is often given to this code.

If the reader will compare the ASCII code set with the special code example above, the incompatibility between a system preparing data in one code and supplying the data to a system using the other code becomes apparent. This brings out the need for translation from one code to another and leads us to a description of how translation is accomplished.

A translation table is prepared and stored in memory. As long as the character sets represented by both codes are identical, the translation process and table are rather simple. By this we mean that if the special code includes a + sign in its character set and the code to which it is to be translated also includes a + sign in its character set, there is a direct relationship that is easily established.

Assume that numbers in the special code are to be translated to ASCII before being recorded on magnetic tape. In this case, the computer reads from memory the first digit in special code. It then uses this digit as a memory address of one location in the translation table. In that location the computer finds the ASCII code for the same digit. It extracts the ASCII code and stores it in an output area and repeats the process for the next digit. When all digits have been translated, the ASCII codes in the output area are recorded on the tape.

A small section of a translation table is shown below to illustrate the process.

MEMORY ADDRESS	CONTENTS OF LOCATION
003	060
004	061
005	062
006	063
007	064

DETECTION OF ERRORS IN THE STORAGE AND TRANSMISSION OF DATA

Whenever data are moved in and out of storage units or between locations, their form is changed somewhat and there is the possibility of errors being introduced. For example, data to be stored on magnetic tape are first converted from the standard signals used within the computer to very small and weak magnetic fields. After this information is recorded, it may be held on the tape for months without being used or changed. Then, during playback, the magnetic fields are converted back to the standard signals and the data are processed. Very simple flaws, such as a buildup of dirt on the recording and reading heads, may cause bits to be changed, so all data-processing equipment provide methods of detecting errors in the storage and transmission of data. The most commonly used methods are discussed below. Most computers use a combination of these methods, although each can be used singly.

Byte, Character, and Word Parity

In this case, a bit called a parity bit is assigned to each of the basic units of information used in the computer and stored or transferred along with that unit. The unit may be a byte, a character, or a word, but for purposes of this explanation, we will assume that it is a byte. When the byte is retrieved from storage, or examined at the receiving station, the information bits are checked and a parity bit is assigned to the combination received, based upon the same scheme by which it was originally assigned. Then the old parity bit is matched against that newly assigned. Obviously they should match and, if they do not, an error has occurred.

An example of the parity-bit scheme appears below. In the left columns, the parity bit is assigned so that the total number of 1s is always odd, while the even-parity scheme makes the total number of 1s even. Note that the scheme provides for only an odd or an even indication. If two errors occur in a byte so that the number of 1s in the byte changes but remains either odd or even, those errors will go undetected.

Bit Position	Contents of the Byte			
0	0	0	0	0
1	0	0	0	0
2	1	0	1	0
3	1	1	1	1
4	0	0	0	0
5	1	1	1	1
6	0	0	0	0
7	1	1	1	1
P	1	0	0	1
	Odd Parity Scheme		Even Parity Scheme	

The parity bit does not leave the circuits supporting the storage medium (memory, disk, or tape). In other words, the parity bit is not carried along with the byte as the byte is handled by the control and arithmetic units. Parity is assigned when the byte is stored, and checked when it is retrieved. The control unit is notified if an error is detected.

When data are transferred long distances, the parity bit is often transmitted along with the byte, to be checked at the receiving station. A disadvantage of the byte-parity checking method is that it significantly increases the number of bits that must be transmitted and thus reduces the transfer rate of the data. It also has the limitation that some communications codes and systems do not have the capability to handle a ninth bit with each byte.

Record or Message Parity

This scheme produces a character at the end of a large unit of information such as a record or message. In this case, the character is composed entirely of parity bits, one corresponding to each bit position in all the characters transferred. Bit 1 of the parity character, for example, is the parity bit for all bit 1s, and is set to odd or even (depending upon the scheme in use) to reflect the total number of 1s transferred through the bit 1 position.

When the information is retrieved from storage or examined at the receiving station, a parity character based upon the data received is formed. It is compared with the parity character received and, of course, they should match.

Special Check Characters

This method involves the addition of one or two characters at the end of a large unit of information such as a record or message block. These characters are most frequently called block check characters (BCC) or cyclic redundancy check (CRC) characters. They are computed before the data are stored or transmitted. Then the same process is performed again when the data are re-

trieved from storage or examined at the receiving station. The newly computed characters are compared with the characters previously attached to the data block. A match indicates that the data were stored or sent without error.

A typical CRC scheme is CRC-16, which is so named because it operates on eight-bit characters and is itself made up of two eight-bit characters. In this case, the numeric value of all the data in the block is treated as a dividend and is divided by a constant. The quotient is discarded, and the sixteen-bit remainder becomes two eight-bit characters placed at the end of the data.

Check Sum

This term means a "sum" of all the information handled as a block that is used to "check" that the block was stored or transferred correctly. Assume, for example, that the computer produced a large block of data as a result of its processing and was going to place this block in permanent storage. In the check-sum method, the computer adds up all the elements in the data block and arrives at the check sum. Overflow would occur many times, of course, but the check-sum number would be a unique number, one that could only be arrived at by following the same procedure with the same data that originally produced it.

The check sum is then attached to the block of data and stored along with the data. When the data block is retrieved from storage, the computer again adds every data element it received from storage and arrives at a sum. It compares this new check sum with the check sum retrieved from storage. If they are identical, the information was transferred and stored correctly.

COMPUTER CONSTRUCTION

Computers are enclosed in upright cabinets, desklike cabinets, or small tabletop units; the enclosures give no hint of what is inside. Only the peripheral units, with their unique shape or special identifying features, such as tape reels, reveal their function at a glance. This section, which deals with internal construction, may be of interest to some readers, particularly those concerned with computer repair.

The first point to consider is that the internal construction of computers does not vary a great deal from one manufacturer to the next. They are surprisingly alike because most computer manufacturers buy the basic component, the integrated circuit "chip," from one of the major chip manufacturers. Integrated-circuit technology is so complex, costly, and fast-changing that computer builders would not want to design and manufacture their own unless they used extremely large numbers of chips. So most builders begin with chips that are commercially available to all.

The next step in construction is called "logic design." Engineers determine how the chips should be interconnected so as best to meet the goals of the computer to be built.

Once the logic design is completed, the builder knows how the chips must be interconnected and goes about doing so. First, the chip package must be considered. The most common chip now in use is a small rectangle with two rows of pins, one on each side of the rectangle, so that the circuits inside the chip can be connected to other chips. This shape is called the dual inline package, or DIP.

Like the old vacuum tubes in a television set, which have pins in their base to plug into a socket, the chip is designed to fit into a socket. Connections are then made to the socket in order to connect the chip to other chips.

At the next step, differences in construction from one builder to another start to appear. A "board" is chosen next, and sockets are mounted in it. The number of sockets and therefore the number of chips on a board vary a good deal from one builder to the next. A board a foot long and 8 inches high might hold 150 chips. Some builders choose small boards and others large for compromises on reasons such as spares costs, ease of replacement, fault location time, etc. A typical board is shown in Figure 58.

How the chips are interconnected with one another is the next major point on which builders differ. There are two primary methods: (1) pins on the back of the board interconnected by wires, and (2) printed circuits on both the front and the back of the board. A printed circuit is a very thin deposit of metal that is used as a wire.

Each method has advantages and disadvantages. Printed circuits are hard to design and costly to change but, once designed, they take up very little space and can be produced quickly in large numbers. Pins and wires, on the other hand, require less design and are easy to change, but they can only be wired slowly and take up considerably more space than printed circuits.

Because of the similarity in board appearance, only a technician or an engineer experienced on a specific computer would be able to recognize a control-unit board from an arithmetic-unit board. When one opens the cabinet on a large computer, all that is visible are the edges of many boards. Most builders supply a locator diagram to

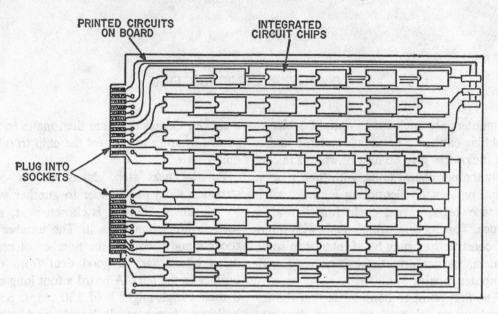

Figure 58. A Printed Circuit Board Used in Computers

point out where specific boards are located.

Next to be discussed is how the boards are interconnected with one another to form a computer. All the signals that must go from board to board are carried by printed circuits that terminate in pins on one side or end of the board. (We will assume that the printed-circuit method of board construction is used.) The board is then plugged into a matching socket mounted in a computer frame, and the sockets are interconnected by either wires or printed circuits like those described above. Shown in Figure 59 is an example of the construction of one chassis. This shows the sockets on the back of the chassis, and printed circuits are used to interconnect the boards in this example.

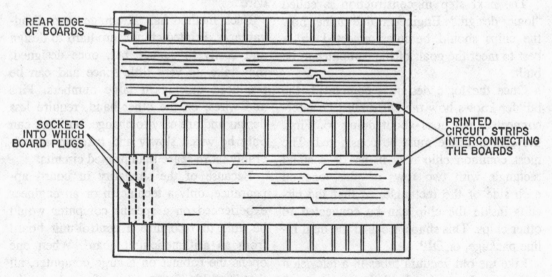

Figure 59. Rear View of a Computer Chassis

The next question then develops: How does a technician locate faults and make repairs? Obviously he must have been trained to do so, but there must also be some kind of "map" showing how the computer is organized and is intended to function. This "map" is provided by "logic" diagrams and interconnection diagrams.

A logic diagram is one in which the function of each chip is represented by a special symbol, and the printed circuits that interconnect them are represented by lines. Pins through which this board is connected to others are represented by a variety of symbols, depending upon the manufacturer. Assume for this discussion that an arrowhead is used, as shown in the section of a logic diagram appearing in Figure 60.

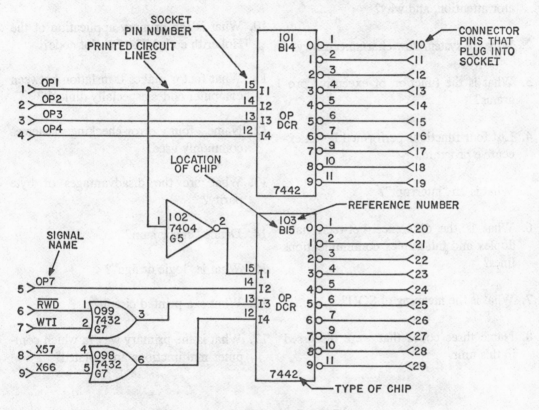

Figure 60. Section of a Logic Diagram

Connections between boards, whether by wires or by printed circuits, are usually provided in the form of lists, often called "back-panel wiring lists." An interconnection diagram is then provided to show where the boards are used and where the wiring lists appear.

Diagnostic programs are the primary ways in which failures are isolated. The programs exercise the equipment by causing it to perform all its intended functions, usually beginning with the basic functions and working toward the most complex. The results of each test are reported to the technician, either through a display or a printout. Operating instructions provided with the program, the results of the test, and interconnection and logic diagrams are then interpreted by the technician to isolate the failure to a board or an interconnection fault.

Boards are usually not repaired at the

computer installation; they are simply replaced in their entirety, with little time spent in isolating a failure to a specific chip. The tools and special equipment necessary to make board repairs are normally available only at a board-repair depot.

QUIZ ON THE SUBJECT MATTER IN UNIT 5

1. What units in the typical computer installation would normally require operator attention, and why?

2. Why are system flow charts necessary?

3. What is the function of executive programs?

4. List four functions performed by an executive program.

5. What is an "interrupt"?

6. What is the difference between half-duplex and full-duplex communications lines?

7. What is the meaning of SOH?

8. Name three codes that were discussed in this unit.

9. Why is it important that a computer system use one of the standard codes?

10. What is the primary application of the Hollerith code? The Baudot code?

11. What factor makes translation between computer codes especially difficult?

12. Name four error-checking schemes commonly used.

13. What are the disadvantages of byte parity?

14. Define "check sum."

15. What is "logic design"?

16. What is a printed circuit?

17. What is the primary way in which computer malfunctions are isolated?

ANSWERS

ANSWERS

UNIT 1

1. a. 0 and 1
   b. 0, 1, 2, 3, 4, 5, 6, and 7
   c. 0, 1, 2, 3, 4, 5, 6, 7, 8, and 9
   d. 0, 1, 2, 3, 4, 5, 6, 7, 8, 9, A, B, C, D,
   E, F (any six letters are acceptable)

2. a. 020
   b. 573
   c. 126
   d. 315
   e. 107
   f. 377

3. a. 43
   b. 243
   c. 170
   d. 116
   e. 192

4. 0000 (0)
    0001 (1)
    0010 (2)
    0011 (3)
    0100 (4)
    0101 (5)
    0110 (6)
    0111 (7)
    1000 (8)
    1001 (9)
    1010 (10)
    1011 (11)
    1100 (12)
    1101 (13)
    1110 (14)
    1111 (15)
    10000 (16)

5. a. DO
   b. EF
   c. 45
   d. 7A
   e. 07

6. Because 0 and 1 can easily be represented by the "off" and "on" states of
   electronic components.

7. a. The output is active if any one of the
      inputs is active.
   b. The output is active only if all inputs
      are active.
   c. The output is inactive only if all
      inputs are active.
   d. The output is inactive if any one of
      inputs is active.

8. a. 10011   9. a. 0000
   b. 1111   b. 0100
   c. 10001   c. 0000
   d. 1110   d. 1001
   e. 1100   e. 1000

10. a. 1111   11. a. 1000
    b. 0111   b. 1101
    c. 1110   c. 0100
    d. 1101   d. 1001
    e. 1111   e. 1000

12. Fixed-point arithmetic is faster and re-
    quires less complex equipment, but it
    imposes the burden of "scaling" on the
    user.

Floating-point arithmetic is slower and requires more complex equipment, but it is easier to use.

13. A byte is made up of eight bits.

14. Groups of records are usually organized into files.

15. Memory unit—stores instructions and data
    Arithmetic unit—manipulates numbers and performs calculations
    Control unit—decodes instructions to control other units
    Input and output units—transfer data and programs in and out of the computer

16. By reflective strips called beginning-of-tape and end-of-tape marks.

17. To allow starting and stopping space between records.

18. To allow the tape to be started and stopped without being broken or over-run.

19. "On line" means immediately accessible to the computer or in the normal flow of computer operations. "Off line" means not immediately available to the computer or not in the normal flow of operations.

20. To protect them from contamination by dirt, fingerprints, etc.

21. Top-load, single platter. Top-load, multiple platter. Front-load, single platter.

22. Matrix and line.

23. To control movement of the paper upward through the printer, relieving the computer of direct-line counting and control.

24. The serial method is slower but uses simpler connections. The parallel method is much faster but requires more cabling.

UNIT 2

1. To store the computer instructions and operating data while they are in use.

2. A read or write command and the address to be used.

3. The contents of the selected memory location are left undisturbed when they are read.

4. 16,384, numbered 0 through 16,383 (decimal).

5. a. 17777
   b. 37777

6. To manipulate numbers and perform the arithmetic operations.

7. To hold one of the quantities involved in an arithmetic or logical operation and to hold the result when the operation is complete.

8. A register that holds the multiplier dur-

ing multiplication and the quotient during division.

9. A quantity twice the length of the basic unit of information used by the computer. When multiplication of two eight-bit quantities is performed, a sixteen-bit, double-length product is formed.

10. Flexibility in using the instructions. For example, more than one accumulator can be maintained if necessary.

11. To act as a counter for repetitive operations, the count most often being used to modify the address of data to be operated on.

12. Instructions to perform repetitive operations need to appear only once, saving memory space.

13. To decode instructions and to manipulate the other computer units so as to carry out the instructions.

14. An operation code and an operand, which is most often a memory address.

15. To hold the memory address of the next instruction to be executed.

16. A "branch," or "jump."

17. The computer is much faster than the peripheral units.

18. To provide temporary storage for data being exchanged between a peripheral unit and the computer memory.

19. It allows the control unit to continue to execute instructions during most of the I/O operation. Only when the control unit and the I/O controller both require the use of memory simultaneously is the control unit interrupted.

20. To load and unload the data-buffer register in response to the ability of the tape and memory to provide or accept data.

UNIT 3

1. The instructions to be included in the set are chosen so that they match as closely as possible the intended use of the computer. (The reader should note that the instruction set covered in Unit 3 is that of a general-purpose machine.)

2. It is a "shorthand" symbol that can be written quickly yet can be easily understood.

3. Operation code and operand.

4. The number of digits required to represent all combinations used in the instruction set, which, of course, is determined by the number of instructions in the set.

5. Usually, the number of memory locations that must be addressed because that is most often the largest number held in the operand field.

6. "N" means that a number will be placed in the position occupied by "N," but that number is variable, not fixed.

7. The operation code numbers are usually in a consecutive series. This is done for ease of decoding and mechanization within the computer.

8. "X" indicates that some number occupies those positions but that number is of no significance—it may be any number and has no effect. Hence "X" means a "don't care" position.

9. The instruction-address counter holds the address of the next instruction to be executed, but the computer will not resume operation without manual intervention. The results of the instruction executed prior to the halt instruction are left undisturbed by the halt instruction.

10. Load-class instructions move information into a specific register, usually from memory, while store-class instructions move the contents of a specific register into a memory location.

11. Since multiplication and division are basically successive additions, subtractions, and shifts, the load, add, subtract, shift, and store instructions could be placed in the proper order and repeated a specific number of times to obtain the same results as a multiply or a divide instruction.

12. To isolate and then test an unknown quantity.

13. Immediately before or after a series of repetitive operations being executed by the computer is performed one time.

14. A closed shift is one in which bits leaving one end of a register or registers reenter the other end so that no bits are lost. An open shift allows bits to leave a register without returning, and it leaves vacated positions in the register.

15. To cause an instruction to be performed out of sequence by replacing the contents of the instruction-address counter with a new address.

16. They provide an automatic record of the "came from" address and an automatic return to the "came from" address thus relieving the programmer of the burden of maintaining a record of all this information.

17. Independent I/O controllers require more information to get started than can be held in a single instruction word, and the IOCC scheme provides a very flexible way in which the control unit can provide this information.

UNIT 4

1. To select and place in the proper order the instructions required to cause a computer to perform a specific task.

2. The binary representations of instructions and addresses used within the computer.

3. To convert the programmer's statements to a machine-code program that can be executed by the computer.

4. Yes, the compiler is usually thought of as a more powerful program. It can perform more functions in response to

a source statement than can an assembler.

5. It separates fields of information and informs the assembler/compiler that a field has ended.

6. A symbolic form is normally used, and the absolute addresses are assigned by the assembler/compiler.

7. The complete, executable program produced by the assembler/compiler system.

8. An item, sequence, or line number is assigned to each source statement in the order in which they are entered.

9. The accuracy of much of the source statement can be checked while it is being entered, and assistance and prompting can be provided by the system.

10. It assists the programmer by establishing the format of the statements he can enter.

11. (1) A source list, (2) a source tape or other form of file such as a disk, (3) an object list, and (4) an object tape or other form of file such as a disk.

12. Subroutine, routine, program, operating system.

13. They organize the functions to be performed and assist the programmer in visualizing the steps required by the job.

14. To allow an individual with limited training to communicate his requirements to a computer.

15. A set of machine-language instructions that carry out the action required by an instruction given in a high-level language.

16. *Problem A*

LDA;RECIN	Load the accumulator with the record number.
TLJ+1;050	Test the accumulator against 050.
BRU;RETAPE	Number was not 50; jump did not take place. Read next record.
BRU;SORT	Number was 50; jump took place and BRU;RETAPE was skipped.

Problem B

LDA;RECIN+17	Load the accumulator with the deduction byte.
SHL;2	Accumulator is shifted left 2 positions, eliminating bits 6 and 7.
SHR;7	Accumulator is shifted right 7 positions, eliminating bits 0 through 4 and retaining only bit 5.
BRZ;TEFUND	Bit 5 was a 0, no deduction for savings bonds.
BRU;SAVDED	Bit 5 was a 1, make deduction for this employee.

Problem C

TIX1;100	Test index register for 100.
BRU;RETAPE	Contents were not 100, no skip took place.
BRU;CALTOT	Contents were 100, BRU;RETAPE was skipped.

Problem D

STO;RECIN+15	Store most significant portion from accumulator.

STQ;RECIN+16	Store least significant portion from MQ register.

Problem E

LDA;RECIN+17	Places byte 17 in the accumulator.
IOR;+RETMK	OR's retirement mask with current deductions, adding retirement.
STO;RECIN+17	Stores updated deduction record.

UNIT 5

1. a. Operator console, to control use of the system.
   b. Tape units, to load and unload tape reels.
   c. Disk units, to load and unload disk packs.
   d. Card reader, as necessary to load cards.
   e. Printer, as necessary to load paper and read the printout.
   f. Data sets (telephones), as necessary to make voice contact and switch to the automatic mode.

2. To organize both the program or programs and the procedure for handling the jobs.

3. To manage the computer's resources in response to job demands.

4. Allocate memory areas, call programs in response to demands, allocate mass storage areas, link programs to one another.

5. Notification to the control unit that a condition has arisen that requires attention.

6. There is only one line available in half duplex, so information can flow in only one direction at any one time. Full duplex provides one line for sending and another for receiving.

7. Start of header, which means a label of some kind.

8. ASCII, EBCDIC, Hollerith, excess 3, BCD.

9. For compatibility of data files with other systems, and to eliminate the need for translation from one code to another.

10. Punched cards and related equipment. Teletypewriter equipment.

11. Differences in character sets.

132

Answers

12. Byte parity, record parity, check sum, cyclic redundancy characters.

13. a. Two errors of the same type in a single byte will go undetected.
   b. Some systems are not equipped to handle the parity bit sent along with a byte or other even divisions of information such as a thirty-two-bit word.
   c. The transmission of a parity bit reduces the rate of information transfer in some systems.

14. The arithmetic sum of all data in a given block, without regard to overflow.

15. The interconnection of basic computer elements, usually integrated-circuit chips today, to cause these elements to perform the functions required for a specific application.

16. A thin, narrow deposit of metal that substitutes for a wire.

17. Diagnostic programs that exercise the computer circuits and report the results to a technician.

GLOSSARY OF TERMS

GLOSSARY OF TERMS

Absolute Address. Usually associated with memory locations, absolute address means the address by which the machine will select a specific location in memory without further address modification. It is the final numeric address of a memory location as opposed to a symbolic name or a number that requires change before it is used to select a memory location.

Absolute Value. The value of a number without regard to its sign.

Access Time. Applies to storage devices, and means the interval between a request for access to a specific storage location and the availability of the contents of that location.

Accumulator. A central register in the arithmetic unit, usually holding one of the operands involved in arithmetic and holding the results when arithmetic is completed. The register whose contents the computer usually operates on and to which most arithmetic-class instructions apply.

Acknowledgment. Any signal or message that indicates the receipt of data or commands. Usually associated with data communications where it means that the message just sent was received correctly.

Adder. The portion of the arithmetic unit where the addition of binary numbers takes place, but adders also perform the logical operations as well.

Address Modification. Any process by which the address specified in an instruction is changed before being applied to memory. Addition of the contents of an index register to a base address specified by an instruction is an example of address modification.

Address Register. A register that holds a memory address before the address is forwarded to memory.

Application Program. The program that *applies* the computer to a specific task for which the computer is intended. A program that causes a computer to print bank statements is an application program, but a program that detects and isolates computer faults is not.

Arithmetic Unit. The core of the computer where most arithmetic operations, logical operations, and testing of results are done.

Array. Applied to memories, array means the overall organization of memory. It might be said that a memory is an 8-bit-by-4096-location array. In general, however, array means a group of items organized into a pattern.

Assembler Program. The program that translates statements made in a symbolic language by a programmer into the machine-language program that the computer executes.

Asynchronous. Applied to two units of the computer, asynchronous means that each is operating at its own rate and that their operations are not synchronized. An I/O controller, for example, can operate asynchronously with respect to the control unit except to notify each other when certain operations are required. In data communications, asynchronous operation means that the sending and receiving units do not maintain common timing. Characters are sent between units complete with information necessary to start and stop the receiving unit.

Backspace. Associated with magnetic tape units, backspace means to back up one record and stop.

Backup Copy. A second copy of the same data in case the primary copy is destroyed. For example, important information stored on disks for daily operation may also be stored on magnetic tapes, but the tapes would be copied onto the disks only if the original information was lost.

Baud. A rate of information transfer over communication lines, roughly equivalent to bits per second but with minor differences. Expressed as 1600 baud, 4800 baud, etc. Derived from *Baudot* code.

Baudot Code. A standard teletypewriter code named after the French postal telegraph engineer. Five information bits make up each character.

BCD (Binary Coded Decimal). An arrangement in which a certain number of bits are intended to be read as a group representing a single decimal digit. Most often four bits are used to represent the decimal digit.

Bi-stable. Any electronic component having only two stable states but most often called a flip-flop or latch and having states called set and reset.

Bit. The contraction of the words "binary digit," but is also used to mean the position

that holds a binary digit, such as bit 5, which means bit *position* 5.

Block. Data or storage locations handled as a group.

Bootstrap. Derived from the saying "to pull himself up by his bootstraps," in computers this usually means a short program capable of loading a large program into memory in response to the operator pushing a "load" switch. Such a program is called a bootstrap loader.

Branch. Instructions in a computer program are performed in sequential order unless a branch instruction causes a departure from this sequence. Equivalent to a *branch* leaving the trunk of a tree.

Buffer. Most commonly used to mean a temporary storage area for data being moved between two locations. May mean a single register or a group of many registers.

Byte. A group of eight bits handled as a unit is the generally accepted meaning of byte, but some also call smaller groups bytes.

Calling. To select a program for execution by stating its name or symbol. The program size varies from a subroutine to a very large program.

Capstan. The small cylindrical device or shaft that spins and moves the tape in a magnetic-tape unit. The capstan actually touches the tape to move it, and the supply and take-up reels move only after the capstan has moved the tape out of the storage loops.

Carry. The digit that exceeds the capacity of a bit position and thus must be combined in the next higher order bit position. When the sum of the quantities in one bit position exceeds "1" in binary arithmetic, a carry of "1" must be inserted into the bit position to the left.

Character. A character is one of the set of symbols handled by the computer. Each letter of the alphabet may be included in the character set, as are numerals, punctuation, and special symbols. There are also control characters included in many character sets; these cause actions and are not shown on display screens and printers. Each character in the character set is represented by a unique binary code.

Check Digit. A digit produced for the purposes of verifying correct storage and transfer of the number to which it is attached. A parity bit is a check digit. There are several methods of arriving at a check digit but all are based upon determining the contents of the number or numbers to which the check digit is attached and assigning the value of the check digit so that it has a fixed relationship to the contents.

Check Sum. An expansion of the check-digit scheme, check sum is the sum of all data handled as a block, without regard to overflow. The check sum is attached to the data block when it is stored or transferred.

Clock. An electronic timing circuit in a computer. A "clock" produces signals on which all computer operations are based.

Codes. Within a computer, a set of binary digits organized so as to represent higher-level functions or symbols; 101111 might always be used to represent an "A," for example, and 00111010 might be the operation code for an ADD instruction.

Compiler. Similar to an assembler program listed earlier, a compiler program also translates statements made by a programmer into machine language. However, a compiler is usually more powerful than an assembler in that the assembler translates on a one-for-one basis, one programmer statement for one machine instruction, but a compiler is capable of translating one programmer statement into several machine instructions. In other words, the compiler can expand the input while an assembler can not.

Complements. Simply, the complement of a number is the value which when added to the number will produce the highest symbol that can be held in each position in the numbering system used. The complement of 44 in the decimal system is 55, resulting in 99, the highest symbols in the numbering system. In the binary system, the complement of 010 is 101, resulting in 111, the highest symbols that can be represented in this system.

Conditional Jump Instructions. Instructions that test for the presence of a certain condition in the computer and, upon finding it, jump to an instruction not in sequential order rather than performing the following instruction.

Control Unit. One of the basic units in all general-purpose computers, the control unit decodes instructions and causes them to be carried out.

Control Word. Usually a supplement to an instruction, a control word holds information that a unit needs to further define the operation required. A control word may also be appended to blocks of data to give important information regarding the content and handling of the data.

Conversational Mode. A computer operating so as to accept English or "near English" statements directly from the user, normally from a keyboard/display unit, and to provide an immediate response that has meaning to the user without translation.

Core Memory. Nearly obsolete as of this writing, core memory was once the primary storage device used within a computer. Tiny circles of magnetic material, organized into large arrays, each provided storage for one bit of information. When the circle, or "core," was magnetized in one direction, it held a "1," and when magnetized in the other direction, it held a "0." Core memory was so dominant that the word "core" is still often used to mean memory, although most memories are now banks of integrated circuits.

Counter. (1) A computer circuit that maintains a sequential binary count, such as the instruction address count. (2) Any temporary storage location in which a program is maintaining a count.

CRT (Cathode Ray Tube). The display device used in most display screens. A vacuum tube that uses an electron beam to excite an internal coating that glows. A TV picture tube is a CRT.

Cursor. A special indicator placed on a display screen to point out the character or position that is the subject of attention. If the display screen and keyboard are being used by the operator to enter information, the cursor points out the next entry position.

Cyclic Redundancy Check. A checking scheme in which all the data being considered as a block are processed by a complex mathematical equation and one or two check characters formed as a result. The check characters are then attached to the data block when it is stored or transferred. The receiving unit or the unit retrieving the data block performs the same mathematical operation on the data block and compares its CRC characters with those received to check the accuracy of transmission or storage.

Data Base. Usually a large collection of information maintained permanently, or semi-permanently, on which a computer is to operate. Examples of a data base are the payroll records of a company and a list of all the parts maintained in its inventory.

Data Link. A communications link over which computer data are transferred. This may range from voice-grade telephone lines

that handle data transfer at low rates to radio links capable of very high rates of transfer.

Debug. To remove the "bugs" from equipment or programs during the initial testing of these products. A "bug" is usually thought of as a design flaw that prevents the equipment or program from fulfilling its intended function rather than a malfunction that occurs after the system has been tested.

Decision Instruction. An instruction whose action depends upon the conditions it finds existing when it is executed. A Branch on 0 instruction, for example, will branch if it finds that the accumulator contents are 0 but will not branch if they are not 0.

Decrement. (1) To reduce a quantity by a specific number, or (2) the number by which the quantity is reduced. When a 1 is subtracted from the contents of an index register, that register is said to have been decremented by 1.

Diagnostic Program. A program intended to test computer equipment and, through a logical process of testing and elimination, isolate failures to small sections of the machine.

Digital. A computer in which all quantities are represented by discrete numbers rather than variations in voltage or current level. A computer that uses voltage and current levels to represent quantities is an analog computer.

Disk Memory. The storage area maintained on magnetic disk units.

Double Precision. A scheme in which the results of an arithmetic operation have twice the number of positions of the individual quantities involved so as to be more precise.

Down Counter. A computer circuit that is originally set to a number and then counts toward zero. A program may also establish a memory location as a counter and reduce its contents, producing a down counter.

Drum Memory. The storage area maintained on magnetic drum units.

Dump. Usually means the copying of memory contents to another storage medium or displaying or printing them for examination. Dump implies the lack of discrimination among the data transferred. In other words, copying is not selective.

Encoder. A device or program that converts one form of information to another. For example, an encoder would convert an "A" to the binary representation to an "A," while a decoder would translate the binary representation and produce an "A."

End-around-carry. A carry from the most significant position of the adder that is brought back to the least significant position and added in when subtraction is done with the subtrahend represented in one's complement form. Use of the 2's complement form does not eliminate the end-around-carry but allows it to be discarded rather than added in the least significant adder stage.

End of File. A special mark recorded in storage media that designates the end of a group of records that is to be considered a file.

Excess 3 Code. A code in which the decimal value of the binary representation of a decimal digit is three greater than the digit itself. For example, the digit 0 is represented by binary 011, read "3" in decimal, but when 011 is translated it produces a 0 on the printer and display screen.

Executable. Applied to programs, executable means a program that can be performed by the computer rather than a source program that must be assembled or compiled before it can be executed. An executable program is usually called an "object" program.

Executive. The name usually given to a program whose function is to control the jobs to be performed and to select the programs required to perform them. An executive would also manage the storage media as required to provide input data and to store processed data.

File. A group of records organized so as to be treated as a unit. All the records in a file hold information that is of the same general type.

Fixed-point Arithmetic. The arithmetic operations performed in a computer in which the position of the binary point is established by the computer design and is not subject to change.

Floating-point Arithmetic. The arithmetic operations performed in a computer in which the position of the binary point in a number is specified by a point position indicator section attached to each number.

Flow Chart. A method by which certain symbols are used to show the functions that a program is to perform and the order in which these functions are to be performed. Decisions to be made, inputs required, outputs produced, and actions to be taken are among the functions shown in program flow charts.

Full Adder. A complete adder capable of handling a carry-in to each stage, forming the sum of two numbers, and producing a carry-out of each stage. See "adder" earlier, and "half adder" following.

Half Adder. The portion of an adder that handles only the two numbers being added and produces a sum and a carry-out. A half adder does not handle a carry-in.

Header. Identifying or labeling information that precedes the data.

Hexadecimal Numbering System. A system in which four binary digits are read as a decimal digit, 0 through 9, and six letters, usually A through F. Counting progresses 0, 1, 2, 3, 4, 5, 6, 7, 8, 9, A, B, C, D, E, F. A total of sixteen combinations are used; therefore the name hexadecimal is given to this system.

Hollerith Code. A code used in punched cards in which one column of twelve positions each is read as a unit. The combination of punches in these twelve positions is the Hollerith code. Named for Dr. Herman Hollerith.

Increment. (1) To increase a quantity by a specific number, or (2) the number by which the quantity is increased. When a 1 is added to the contents of an index register, for example, that register is said to have been incremented by 1.

Index Register. A register, usually in the arithmetic unit, that holds a count. The most common use of this count is to modify memory addresses so that the same operations can be performed repeatedly but with a different memory address each time.

Indexing. Generally means the modification of a memory address by the contents of an index register. Can also mean a system of electronic record-keeping in which an index of the contents of a file is maintained.

Indirect Addressing. Normally, the address portion of an instruction is the address of the data to be operated on. However, indirect addressing is a method by which the address portion of an instruction directs the control unit to a memory location in which the address of the data to be operated on is held. In other words: "Go to this address to get your final address."

Instruction Register. Always part of the control unit, the instruction register holds each instruction after it is read from memory and while it is being decoded and executed.

Instruction Word. This means an instruction consisting of an operation code, speci-fying what is to be done, and an operand, which is a quantity to be used in the execution of the instruction.

Integrated Circuit. Circuits formed so that their components cannot be separated. Usually called "chips" because they are very small and are composed of materials such as silicon.

Interrupt. A signal used by other computer units to gain the attention of the control unit. Usually produced in response to important external conditions, an interrupt signal produces a break in the flow of activities. Action taken in response to the interrupt varies according to the programs being executed, but the immediate needs of the external device are normally met before the control unit returns to the point at which it was interrupted.

Keypunch. (1) The equipment used to translate data into coded form acceptable to a computer or (2) the action of operating the equipment to accomplish the translation. Older systems used equipment that actually punched the data into cards as an operator read the data from input sheets and typed the data at a keyboard. However, modern systems convert the keyboard input directly to electronic form.

Lateral Parity. Usually means the individual parity bit assigned to a single byte or character.

Logic Diagram. The method of representing the circuits that make up a computer by symbols that illustrate the function of each circuit.

Longitudinal Parity. A parity character formed at the end of a block of data. Each bit in the parity character represents the total parity of all preceding bits of the same level. For example, bit 1 of the parity character is the parity bit for bit 1 of all preceding characters.

Longitudinal Redundancy Check Character (LRCC). Usually associated with magnetic-tape units, LRCC means the longitudinal parity characters recorded at the end of a block of data, normally at the end of a file.

Loops. Applies to programs, and means a group of instructions that return to the starting point and repeat themselves, usually until a certain event takes place to break the loop.

Machine Code. The binary numbers used within the computer to represent instructions, addresses, numbers, and other characters. Most often, however, machine code is more narrowly defined to mean the binary representation of the operation code portion of an instruction.

Macro Instruction. (1) A source statement that causes at least several instructions to be generated. (2) A "large" instruction that may call for routines or programs to be executed.

Matrix. An array of elements in a rectangle, such as the printing pattern of a matrix printer. Also an array of numbers.

Memory. The storage device immediately accessible to the control and arithmetic units of a computer, where the current instructions and operating data are stored.

Memory-address Register. The register, usually in the memory unit, that holds the address applied to the memory array.

Memory Cycle. The functions performed by a memory unit in response to a read or a write command.

Micro Operations. Most often used to mean the individual steps necessary to carry out an instruction. Sometimes associated with micro programming, which means to select the steps and processes to be performed within an instruction.

Microsecond. One one-millionth of a second.

Millisecond. One one-thousandth of a second.

MODEM. An abbreviation for *Modulator-Demodulator*, a device used to convert data from a computer to a form suitable for transmission and back again to computer form. A MODEM, for example, is used at both ends of a voice-grade telephone line when two computers are exchanging data over that line.

Multiple Address. Applies to a computer whose instruction word holds more than one address section. Such a computer is called a multiple-address machine, as opposed to a single-address machine.

Multiplex. To place information from several different sources on a single channel, usually separating them by choosing one source at a time for connection to the channel.

Nanosecond. One one-billionth of a second.

Nondestructive Readout. The process by which data can be read from a storage device without affecting the stored information. This term is usually applied to memory units rather than other storage devices because older memories destroyed the contents of each location read and required that they be restored.

Nonexecutable. Applied to statements entered by a programmer, this means that that statement is not converted to a machine instruction and executed. An example of a nonexecutable statement is "enter remarks."

Nonreturn-to-zero Recording. In magnetic recording devices, the practice of not returning the magnetic field to zero at the end of a bit position.

Object Program. A program that is in machine language and is executed by the computer. It is the "object" of entering and assembling source statements and represents the final results of the process.

Off-line Operation. An operation that is not in the primary flow of computer activities. For example, data from a magnetic tape may be printed out while a computer is not engaged in or available for its primary task. In this case, the computer is doing off-line printing. Can also mean an operation such as a direct connection between the tape and printer, which bypasses the computer completely and is not under computer control. A peripheral unit that is said to be off line is one that is not immediately accessible to the computer.

On-line Operation. The opposite of the off-line operation above, an on-line operation *is in the primary flow* of computer activities. When applied to the status of a peripheral unit, it means that that unit *is immediately accessible* to the computer.

Operand. Usually considered to be one of two major parts of an instruction, the operation code being the other. An operand is an item to be operated upon or is somehow involved in the operation specified by the operation code. An operand may be a memory address, a number to be added, a parameter of some type, etc.

Operation Code. A portion of an instruction or control word that specifies the function that the computer is to perform. Eventually translated into binary-form machine language, the operation code may be any one of several high-level forms, including a symbolic form, when entered by the programmer.

Overflow. The condition resulting from an operation in which the result exceeds the capacity of the computer's basic unit of information to represent it. A decimal 15 could be represented by four bit positions, for example, but if the results of an addition were 16, an overflow would have occurred

and the result is meaningless because it has exceeded the capacity of the basic unit of information.

Parallel. The organization of a unit so that all parts of an element are available at the same time. Usually used to describe the way in which bytes and words are available and operated on. When all eight bits of a byte are made available simultaneously, that is said to be parallel; if they are available only one at a time, that is said to be serial. The word "parallel" also applies to high-level operations, but always has the same basic meaning: simultaneous availability or operation.

Parity Checking. As defined in the dictionary, "parity" has to do with maintaining equality. Applied to computer use, it means adding a bit to a unit of information so as to maintain the total number of 1s in that unit always odd or always even, depending upon which method is chosen. The bit added is called the parity bit, and it is a way of checking the accuracy of storage or transfer.

Polling. A scheme in which a central unit chooses one remote unit after another and exchanges data with each remote unit that has information ready. Usually associated with a central computer and many remote terminals.

Positional Notation. The assignment of different weights to the positions that a digit in any numbering system occupies, such as the units, tens, and hundreds positions in the decimal system. The weight of a specific character depends upon the position that it occupies. Contrast this with the confusing positions used by the Roman numeral system.

Program. (1) A collection of computer instructions arranged so as to cause the computer to perform a specific task. (2) The act of selecting and placing in the proper order the instructions required.

Protocol. Most often associated with the exchange of data between two systems separated by considerable distance, protocol means the rules and conventions that will be followed by each system during the exchange.

Pseudo Instruction. An instruction issued as a source statement by the programmer but that is not executed by the computer directly on a one-machine instruction for one pseudo-instruction basis. An example of a pseudo instruction might be "title the page, TTP," which would be converted to many machine instructions in order to carry out that act.

Queue. Usually a number of inputs placed in order to be processed in sequence, but can also apply to a number of units awaiting output. The first group would be called the "input queue" and the latter the "output queue." It should be noted that the elements placed in a queue are usually large— messages between computer sites, for example—rather than just a few bytes to be processed one after another.

Radix. The quantity of characters in a numbering system. The radix of the binary system is 2; two characters, 1 and 0, make up the system. The radix of the decimal system is 10, the ten characters being 0 through 9.

Random Access. The ability to gain access to any one storage location among many in an equal amount of time and effort and not depending upon any previous action. Tape units, for example, are serial access rather than random access. Usually only the memory within the computer is thought of as being a random-access storage unit.

Reading. The retrieval of information from some form of storage.

Read-only Memory. A storage unit whose contents cannot be changed during normal operation. In other words, data cannot be written into this memory by the computer; it was placed there in advance by a special means, and the computer can only read the memory contents. Read-only memories have the advantage of being very small and requiring a minimum of supporting circuits.

Read/Write Head. A small unit capable of both producing and sensing magnetic fields. Used to record and play back information on magnetic tapes, disks, drums, and any other magnetic recording device.

Real-time Processing. The processing of data from an event when the event is actually occurring rather than storing the data for processing later. An example of real-time processing would be a machine tool being operated by a computer in which the progress of the tool was sensed by the computer, and directions given by the computer were based on the tool's progress.

Record. A group of bytes, characters, or words organized and handled as a unit is the narrow definition of "record" used in the computer industry. "Record" is usually applied to the organization of data on magnetic tapes and disks.

Register. A group of bi-stable devices used to hold a unit of information handled by a computer. Most often associated with the groups of bi-stables in the control, arithmetic, and input-output units, but the locations in storage (particularly memory) are called registers by some.

"Scratch Pad" Storage. A very small memory maintained in the arithmetic or control units for the purpose of temporarily storing certain information without using the main memory. This information may be the interim results of calculations or the information required to return from an interrupt.

Serial. The organization of a unit so that only one part of an element is available at a time. (See Parallel.) Used to describe the way in which data are transferred or processed, such as only one bit of a byte being available at a time. To handle or process in sequence rather than simultaneously.

Serial Access. The ability to reach information in storage only sequentially. Tape units are serial-access storage units in that the tape must be moved past the read/write head until the desired location is reached.

Shift Register. A register in which the information can be moved laterally—that is, the register contents can be shifted so that a bit moves to the adjacent position.

Software. Very commonly used to mean programs, while hardware means the equipment, but originally meant the programs, programming aids, and the documentation associated with programs.

Source Program. The statements originally entered by the programmer before they are assembled or compiled. The program written in the source language that is converted to machine code and the object program by an assembler or compiler.

Subroutine. A small group of instructions intended to perform one specific function. Whenever this function is required by a program, the subroutine is called and executed. This allows several different programs to use the same subroutine and avoids the need to include these instructions in every program.

Synchronous. Applied to data communications, synchronous means that the sending and receiving units use a common timing signal to remain "in step" while data are being transferred, and the data stream is continuous. When applied to computers it means that the computer units are related by a common timing cycle and that their operations have a fixed timing relationship to one another.

Time-out. (1) A specific interval in which an event must occur or the operation is con-sidered in error or ended is called a "time-out." (2) The act of allowing this interval to elapse is called a "time-out."

Time Sharing. Generally thought of as the sharing of a large central computer by several parties, usually from remote locations, on the basis of having certain intervals assigned to each party. Sometimes the access is based on demand, and in other cases it is based upon time assignments made in advance.

Trace Routine. A program intended to assist programmers in locating flaws during the program-testing process. A trace routine allows the programmer to execute one instruction at a time in order to examine the results of that instruction, the inputs provided, and the contents of the most significant registers involved. Large-scale computers with elaborate control panels do not require the use of trace routines because the controls and displays available to the programmer enable him to accomplish the same thing. Trace routines are most often used in small computers where the controls and displays available are limited.

Translation. The conversion of one form of code to another. For example, source statements are "translated" to machine language by assemblers and compilers, operation codes are translated into commands by decoders in the control units, and a code such as EBCDIC held in storage is translated to ASCII for transmission to another system.

Transparent. To "see through" predetermined character assignments and view only the binary representation. An example of this is the "transparent mode" of data communications. Until this mode is chosen, the bit patterns are interpreted in a preassigned way, an "END" command might be represented by 10101111, for example, and whenever 10101111 was received the computer would recognize it as the END command. In the transparent mode, the computer receiving 10101111 would simply process it as a number and not interpret it as an END command, thus "seeing through" the preassigned meaning.

User Program. An application program operated by the computer user.

Volume. A large collection of files, usually a large physical division such as a reel of magnetic tape.

Word. One of the basic units of information processed by the computer. Most often, a word is considerably larger than a byte. A computer may use a sixteen-bit, thirty-two-bit, or forty-eight-bit word as its basic unit of information.

Writing. The process of placing information in a storage medium.